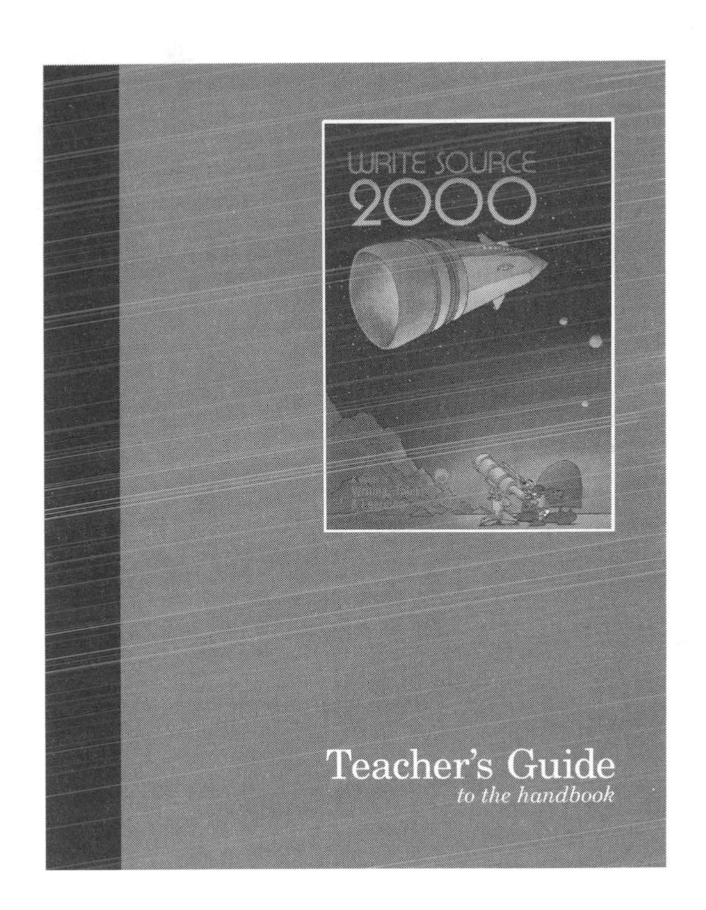

A Teacher's Guide to accompany

Write Source 2000

WRITE SOURCE

GREAT SOURCE EDUCATION GROUP
a Houghton Mifflin Company
Wilmington, Massachusetts

To Middle-School Educators

If you are committed to middle-school education, you are a very special person. It is for you and your students that we have designed our *Write Source 2000* handbook and supporting materials.

This guide will not only help you use our handbook effectively and wisely, but it will also help you review your roots as a teacher. We have tried to address many of the "big questions" teachers are asking today in such a way that this guide will help you integrate your professional experience with current research.

If you have any questions, please call. (Use our toll-free number—1-800-289-4490.) We are always ready to help you or receive your feedback.

The Write Source/Great Source Education Group

Written and Compiled by Pat Sebranek and Dave Kemper

Printed in the United States of America

International Standard Book Number: 0-669-43273-3

3 4 5 6 7 8 9 10 -HLG- 02 01 00 99 98 97 96

What You'll Find Inside

The *Write Source 2000* Student Handbook

Five Contemporary Writing Programs

Teaching Writing

Teaching Reading

Teaching Learning and Thinking

Minilessons to Use with *Write Source 2000*

Using *The Write Source 2000 Language Program*

A Quick Tour

Write Source 2000 serves as the perfect language handbook for middle-school grades, one that will help your students improve their ability **to write** (prewriting through proofreading), **to think** (creatively, logically, and clearly), and **to learn** (in the classroom, in small groups, independently). This quick tour will highlight the five main parts of the handbook.

Write Source 2000
A Quick Tour

The Process of Writing

Students will use this section to answer their questions about writing, from writing to learn to writing as a process, from building paragraphs to combining sentences.

Colorful illustrations and a personal tone make *Write Source 2000* very attractive to students.

003

003 **Writing to Learn**

The Writing Process 011-012

The Writing Process

What we offer you in this section is a good description of what generally goes on during the process of writing. We also offer you plenty of suggestions, guidelines, and insights along the way to help you develop your own writing.

Writing in Action 011

Before we talk about your writing, let's look at the way a professional writes. A professional usually "lifts off" by writing for herself—with only a hint of an idea or plan in mind. Her initial purpose is to explore and discover potential starting points for writing. Once a writer hits upon one that she likes, she's on her way to learn what she can through her writing. And she won't "touch down" until her writing is ready to share with her readers.

"Writing is mind traveling — destination unknown."

What happens to the writing while it's in orbit depends on the project. Usually a writer will write something, read it, change it so some of the ideas are clearer, read it again, ask someone else to read it, make some more changes, and so on. There is a lot of forward and backward motion as a writer tries to make sense out of her writing and shape it for her readers. Writing is called a process because it goes through such a series of changes.

The Steps in the Process 012

We identify four steps in our discussion of the writing process: *selecting, collecting, connecting,* and *correcting*. **Selecting** refers to the process of choosing a subject to explore in writing. **Collecting** refers to all of the searching, gathering, thinking, talking, and planning that goes on during a writing project. (Note that I said during a project. It is ongoing.) **Connecting** refers to all of the writing you do to connect and shape your thoughts into a meaningful composition. **Correcting** refers to those finishing touches which are made as the writing is put into its final form. It includes editing and proofreading.

Helpful HINT: This section is meant to be read and talked about with your classmates. Have a parent or family member read it as well, so they can help you with your writing.

Helpful guidelines and checklists make information easy to find and use.

Combining Sentences 103-104

Guidelines for Sentence Combining

The guidelines which follow will help you transform short, choppy sentences into longer, smoother-reading sentences.

Use a Series of Words and Phrases 103

■ Ideas from shorter sentences can be combined into one sentence using *a series* of words or phrases.

◆ **Shorter sentences:** The cat is soft. The cat is cuddly. The cat is warm.
Combined sentence: The cat is soft, cuddly, and warm. (A series of three words was used to combine the three sentences into one.)

Helpful HINT: All of the words or phrases you use in a series should be parallel—stated in the same way. (All should be nouns or *ing* words or the same in some other way.) Otherwise, your sentences will sound awkward and unbalanced.

◆ **Awkward series:** The dog was friendly, reliable, and he showed exceptional intelligence.
Corrected sentence: The dog was friendly, reliable, and intelligent. (The three items in the series are now parallel. That is, all of the items are single-word adjectives.)

Use Compound Sentences and Compound Verbs 104

■ Ideas from shorter sentences can be combined using *compound subjects* and *compound verbs* (predicates). A compound subject includes two or more subjects in one sentence. A compound verb includes two or more verbs in one sentence.

◆ **Two shorter sentences:** John ran into the glass door. Sarah ran into the glass door.
Combined sentence with compound subject: *John and Sarah* ran into the glass door.

◆ **Two shorter sentences:** Mr. Fingers fumbled with the stack of papers. He dropped them down the stairs.
Combined sentence with compound verb: Mr. Fingers *fumbled* with the stack of papers and *dropped* them down the stairs.

Helpful HINT: As you continue working on your sentence skills, think about how different kinds of words and ideas best fit together. Soon you will be combining these ideas naturally as you write!

2 The Forms of Writing

In this part, students will find guidelines and models for journals, experience papers, reviews, letters, poems, stories, and much more.

129

129

Personal Writing

Writing Poetry

Of all the forms of creative writing, none is more loved/hated than poetry. Many of those who love it have found that poetry allows them to share their thoughts and feelings in a unique way. Others enjoy reading and listening to the rhymes, rhythms, and images of poetry. As to those who "hate" it? Well, they probably haven't tried poetry lately—at least not in the way it is described on the following pages.

What Is Poetry?

221

The poet Marianne Moore defines poetry as "imaginary gardens with real toads in them." This definition may seem unusual to you. When you think of a definition, you probably think of something like "a verb is a word which expresses action or a state of being." Poetry, however, is too creative and exciting to be effectively defined in such a factual way. That is why Ms. Moore chose such a different way to define poetry. She has given life to her definition and invites us to use our imaginations and share in her creation. A poem is an exciting and imaginative creation, an "imaginary garden." Poems come from our real world experiences—the "toads" which hop in and out of our lives every day.

"A poem is an imaginary garden with real toads in it."

"Imaginary gardens" might be new to you, but poetry is not. Your idea of poetry might be an old jump-roping jingle like "I like coffee/ I like tea/ I like the boys/ Do they like me?" Or, it might be the lyrics or words of your favorite song. More than anything, good poetry must present ideas in a new and different way, a way that makes poetry fun to listen to and interesting to read.

Poetry Is Not the Same as Prose

222

As you will see from the samples on the following pages, poetry comes in all shapes and sizes. For many years, it was written in lines and stanzas (groups of lines) and followed a certain pattern of rhyme and rhythm. Today, poetry doesn't have to rhyme. And it is often written with just words and phrases—not lines or sentences. Prose, on the other hand, is the writing you do every day in school, writing in which you use sentences and paragraphs to turn out reports, essays, and stories.

***Write Source 2000* addresses many forms of personal, subject, creative, and research writing.**

The Book Review

A book review is a special type of writing. In a book review, you state your reaction or your opinion about a book (or part of a book) you have read. You then support that opinion with specific facts and details taken from the book. The subject for a book review usually comes from one or more of the four main parts of a book—the *plot*, the *characters*, the *setting*, or the *theme*.

Reading and Understanding Your Book

187

To write a good book review, you need to read a book very carefully. And, you will need to reread those parts of the book you plan to use in your review. Also, you will need to know what kind of book you are reading—modern romance novel, historical novel, science fiction, biography, and so on. It would be wrong to criticize a biography because it lacks action and suspense. A biographer attempts to write about the life of an important person in a special way, a way that helps the reader understand that person better. A biographer isn't trying to write an action-packed story.

Selecting: *Choosing a Topic*

188

Also keep in mind that a review is a type of persuasive writing, writing which includes an opinion supported by facts and details; therefore, you must select an idea which is a statement of opinion for your review.

Use the list of ideas on the next page to help you choose a specific subject for your review. If you are asked to write a one-paragraph review, begin by choosing one of the basic parts of a story *(plot, characters, theme,* or *setting)* to write about. If you are assigned a longer book review, choose related ideas *(theme* and *character*, for example, or two strong characters).

3 The Tools of Learning

When students have a question about studying, reading, speaking, or thinking, they should turn to this section of the handbook for help.

305

305 **Thinking to Learn**

405

Interviewing

One of the most valuable sources of information available to people today is other people. And the best way to get good, current information from other people is to sit down and talk to them and listen to what they have to say. This is what newspaper, magazine, and television people do everyday. You, too, should consider interviewing others whenever you are asked to find information or research a topic. The tips which follow should help make your interview more comfortable and successful.

405 **Tips for Better Interviewing**

Before the Interview . . .

- Select a person to interview who has special knowledge or personal experiences to share.
- Write out all the questions you would like to ask. (Phrase your questions so that your subject cannot answer with just a "yes" or "no.")
- Make an appointment for a time and place which is convenient for the person you are going to interview.
- Let your subject know beforehand what kind of project you are working on and what topics you hope to cover. (You might even tell him or her some of the questions so he or she has time to think about them.)
- Study your topic as much as possible before the interview so that you are not likely to be overwhelmed with new information.
- Practice with your tape recorder beforehand so that you know how to change batteries, tapes, and sides of the tape. Label your tapes ahead of time.
- Also practice asking your questions and writing down responses. (A classmate or family member will be happy to let you practice your interview on him or her.)

Study-Reading Skills 361-364

Study-Reading Skills

If you want to develop all your interests and talents to their fullest, you must be able to read—and read well. Being able to read well is a key to doing well in school and, later, doing well on the job. Luckily, it's never too late to become a better reader. The information in this section of your handbook will help you improve your reading, studying, and learning skills.

What Is a Good Reader? 361

A good reader is a careful, thoughtful reader who understands the reason he or she is reading. A good reader is always looking for ways to improve his vocabulary and knows when and how to use a dictionary or reference book. A good reader knows how to use "context clues" and read between the lines. And, perhaps most importantly, a good reader knows when to simply "enjoy" a good book, and when and how to "study" one.

Techniques for Reading to Learn 362

Much of the reading you will be asked to do in school will involve study-reading, reading which you are expected to remember for a discussion, test, or project. There are many techniques or strategies you can use for these types of reading assignments. Among the most popular are KWL, Mapping, Word Pictures, and SQ3R.

KWL 363

To use the KWL technique, all you need to do is set up a chart similar to the one below and fill it in each time you read. It may seem too simple to be of much help, but you will be surprised how helpful it can be.

K	W	L
List what you KNOW	List what you WANT to know	List what you LEARNED

Mapping 364

A second technique is called "mapping." As the name suggests, you actually draw a map of the reading material. Mapping is much like clustering, but in mapping the ideas come from the reading, not your personal experiences. (Refer to the clustering sample, 035.) Simply place the subject of your reading in the center and "map" out the details as you read.

***Write Source 2000* makes all aspects of language and learning active, enjoyable, and meaningful.**

The Yellow Pages Guide to

Using the Right Word

Here are some tips which will help you "use the right word" whenever you write. **First**, it won't take you long to realize that proper word choice is more important in some situations than in others: for example, it is important in a letter to the editor of the local paper, in a formal essay or research paper, and in a presentation to a local church or civic group. **Second**, you should become familiar with the words which are commonly misused by looking through this section in your handbook. **Third**, you should refer to this section whenever you have a question about which word is the correct one to use. (*Note:* If your handbook doesn't answer your question, refer to a dictionary.) **Finally**, you should make every effort to keep your writing both correct and natural.

574 .... a, an
- *A* is used before words which begin with a consonant sound; *an* is used before words which begin with a vowel sound.

> **a heap, a cat, an idol, an elephant, an honor, a historian**

575 .... accept, except
- The verb *accept* means "to receive"; the preposition *except* means "other than."

> **Melissa graciously *accepted* defeat** [verb]. **All the boys *except* Zach were here** [preposition].

576 .... affect, effect
- *Affect* is always a verb; it means "to influence." *Effect* can be a verb, but it is most often used as a noun. As a verb, *effect* means "to produce or make happen."

> **Mark's giggle *affected* the preacher. Mark's giggle *effected* a pinch from his mother.**

- The noun *effect* means "the result."

> **The *effect* of the pinch was a sore leg.**

allowed, aloud 577
- The verb *allowed* means "permitted" or "let happen"; *aloud* is an adverb which means "in a normal voice."

> **We weren't *allowed* to read *aloud* in the library.**

allusion, illusion 578
- An *allusion* is a brief reference or mention of a famous person, place, thing, or idea. An *illusion* is a false impression or idea.

> **As he made an *allusion* to the great magicians of the past, Houdini created the *illusion* of having sawed his assistant in half.**

a lot 579
- *A lot* is not one word; *a lot* (two words) is a very general descriptive phrase which should be avoided in formal writing.

A **period** is used to end a sentence which makes a statement or a request, or which gives a command which is not used as an exclamation.

> **Try these car facts on for size.** [Command]
>
> **Cars of the future will come with electronic navigation systems.** [Statement]
>
> **Video rearview mirrors will relay the "rear view" on an in-dash video screen.** [Statement]
>
> **Relax.** [Request]
>
> **In-car radar systems (they can scan up to 400 feet) will help you avoid head-on collisions.** [Statement]

Note: It is not necessary to place a period after a statement which has parentheses around it and is part of another sentence.

460 .... After an Initial
- A period should be placed after an initial.

> **M. E. Kerr** [writer]
>
> **Steven P. Jobs** [founder of Apple computers]

461 .... As a Decimal
- Use a period as a decimal point and to separate dollars and cents.

> **Experts are 69.9 percent sure (okay 70 percent) that a pill now**

At the End of a Sentence 462
- When an abbreviation is the last word in a sentence, only one period should be used at the end of the sentence.

> **By the year 2030, a 65-year-old individual may be as fit as a 45-year-old person today because of advances in nutrition, exercise, preventative medicine, etc.**

After Abbreviations 463
- A period is placed after each part of an abbreviation—unless the abbreviation is an acronym. An acronym is a word formed from the first (or first few) letters of words in a set phrase. (See 556.)

> **Abbreviations .... Mr., Mrs., Ms., Dr., A.D., B.C.**
>
> **Acronyms .... BASIC, DOS, laser, modem**

An **ellipsis** (three periods) may be used to indicate a pause in dialogue or to show omitted words or sentences. (When typing, leave one space before, after, and between each period.)

To Show a Pause 465
- An ellipsis is used to indicate a pause in dialogue.

> **"Why did I get home late, Dad? Well, Jill and I . . . ah . . . yeah, were in another galaxy. Well, I . . . ah . . . mean we were watch-**
> **. . . on**

The Yellow Pages Guide to

Understanding Sentences

There is little doubt that the sentence is the cornerstone of all writing. Whether we like it or not, we are expected to use *sentences*—not sentence fragments, run-ons, or spliced sentences—but complete, colorful, concise, correct sentences in a variety of shapes and sizes. As you practice and experiment with your sentences, it might be helpful for you to know how different kinds of sentences are put together and what the various sentence "elements" are. The information in this section should help.

A **sentence** is made up of one or more words which express a complete thought. (*Note:* A sentence begins with a capital letter; it ends with a period, question mark, or exclamation point.)

> **This book should help you write. It explains many things.**
>
> **How do you plan to use it? I hope you find it helpful!**

For more information on sentences, turn to "Composing Sentences," 090-114, in your handbook.

WORDS IN A SENTENCE

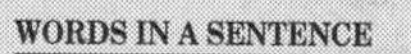

Subject & Predicate 696
- A sentence must have a subject and predicate in order to express a complete thought. Either the subject or the predicate (or both) may *not* be stated, but both must be clearly understood.

> [*You*] **Join our union!** [*You* is the understood subject.]
>
> **Who needs independence? People.** [*do*] [*Do* is the understood predicate.]
>
> **What can you lose by joining?** [*We can lose*] **Freedom.** [*We* is the understood subject, and *can lose* is the understood predicate.]

Subject 697
- A subject is the part of a sentence which is doing something or about which something is said.

> **In 1940 *Russia* took away the independence and identities of the Baltic states. Now *they* are finally regaining their freedom.**

4 The Proofreader's Guide

Punctuation, capitalization, spelling, and the parts of speech are all covered in "The Yellow Pages."

This easy-to-use guide answers all your students' editing and proofreading questions.

The Student Almanac

"The Student Almanac" contains information useful for math, science, and social studies classes.

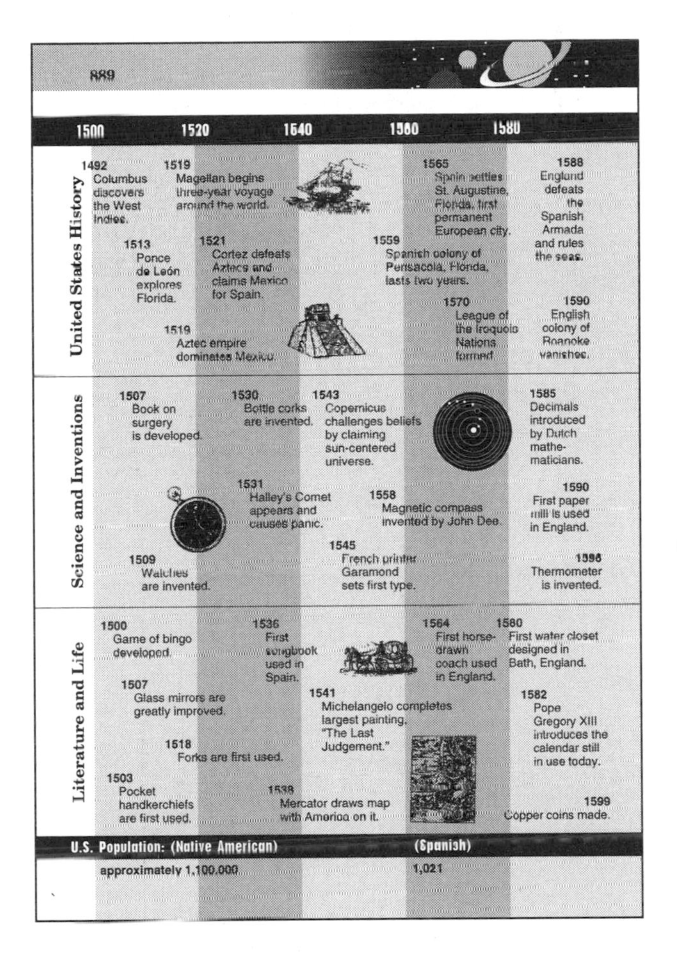

889

	1500	1520	1540	1560	1580
United States History	1492 Columbus discovers the West Indies. 1513 Ponce de León explores Florida.	1519 Magellan begins three-year voyage around the world. 1521 Cortez defeats Aztecs and claims Mexico for Spain. 1519 Aztec empire dominates Mexico.		1559 Spanish colony of Pensacola, Florida, lasts two years. 1565 Spain settles St. Augustine, Florida, first permanent European city. 1570 League of the Iroquois Nations formed.	1588 England defeats the Spanish Armada and rules the seas. 1590 English colony of Roanoke vanishes.
Science and Inventions	1507 Book on surgery is developed. 1509 Watches are invented.	1530 Bottle corks are invented. 1531 Halley's Comet appears and causes panic.	1543 Copernicus challenges beliefs by claiming sun-centered universe. 1545 French printer Garamond sets first type.	1558 Magnetic compass invented by John Dee.	1585 Decimals introduced by Dutch mathematicians. 1590 First paper mill is used in England. 1596 Thermometer is invented.
Literature and Life	1500 Game of bingo developed. 1507 Glass mirrors are greatly improved. 1518 Forks are first used. 1503 Pocket handkerchiefs are first used.	1536 First songbook used in Spain. 1538 Mercator draws map with America on it.	1541 Michelangelo completes largest painting, "The Last Judgement."	1564 First horse-drawn coach used in England.	1580 First water closet designed in Bath, England. 1582 Pope Gregory XIII introduces the calendar still in use today. 1599 Copper coins made.
U.S. Population:	(Native American) approximately 1,100,000			(Spanish) 1,021	

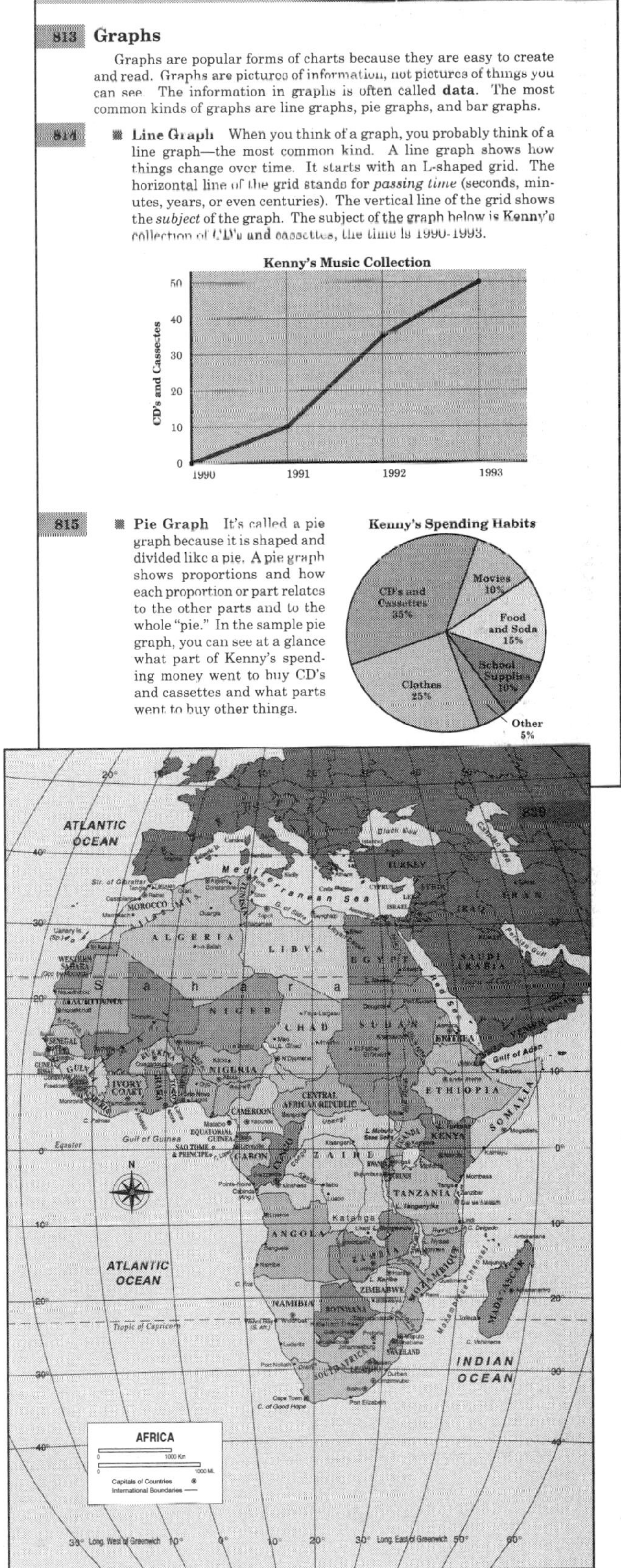

813-815

813 **Graphs**

Graphs are popular forms of charts because they are easy to create and read. Graphs are pictures of information, not pictures of things you can see. The information in graphs is often called **data**. The most common kinds of graphs are line graphs, pie graphs, and bar graphs.

814 ■ **Line Graph** When you think of a graph, you probably think of a line graph—the most common kind. A line graph shows how things change over time. It starts with an L-shaped grid. The horizontal line of the grid stands for *passing time* (seconds, minutes, years, or even centuries). The vertical line of the grid shows the *subject* of the graph. The subject of the graph below is Kenny's collection of CD's and cassettes; the time is 1990-1993.

815 ■ **Pie Graph** It's called a pie graph because it is shaped and divided like a pie. A pie graph shows proportions and how each proportion or part relates to the other parts and to the whole "pie." In the sample pie graph, you can see at a glance what part of Kenny's spending money went to buy CD's and cassettes and what parts went to buy other things.

Full-color maps, a historical time line, the metric system—*Write Source 2000* is truly an all-school handbook!

Introducing the Handbook

The pages that follow can be used to introduce *Write Source 2000* to your students and get them started on the road to becoming active, independent learners.

Using Write Source 2000
Getting Started Activities

The *Write Source 2000* handbook was written by teachers for students. More than anything else, the teachers wanted to put together a handbook that students would like and actually use. Over the past several years, both students and teachers have told us what they like best about the handbook, what they would like to see added or changed, and what they do when the book is first put into the hands of the students. Here are some of the suggestions they sent us:

What would you put in a handbook?

Before you even hand out *Write Source 2000*, ask students what they would put into an all-purpose student handbook if they were in charge of designing one. We have included an activity sheet to help your students design their handbooks. (See "You Have Been Called!") We also have included a follow-up activity that asks students to compare and contrast the handbook they designed with our handbook.

Scavenger Hunts

Another popular idea with both students and teachers is the scavenger hunt. Ask your students to find a random list of items in *Write Source 2000*. (Some should be fairly obvious, some less so.) Create your own lists of items for your students to find or use one of the scavenger hunts we have provided for you (Scavenger Hunt A or B).

- A variation on the scavenger hunt is the "Getting to Know My Handbook" activity. Challenge your students to find suitable words from *Write Source 2000* to fill in the "Getting to Know" chart. The words they choose must begin with the letters in "Write Source."
- Another Variation: Ask students to find one, two, three, or more items in *Write Source 2000* that are interesting and valuable to know, but that are not necessarily obvious or easy to locate. Students can then challenge the class to find these items.
- Still Another Variation: Duplicate and distribute copies of "Easy Liftoff" for an enjoyable and fast-paced handbook search. You might make a contest out of this activity and see who can get the most correct answers in a specified amount of time.

Other Activities

- Give your students the following assignment: Find one page, one short section, one set of guidelines, one illustration, one model, one important fact, or one quotation you find interesting, entertaining, stimulating, valuable, etc. Students should prepare to share their discoveries with members of their discussion group or with the entire class.
- Give your students 10 minutes to page through *Write Source 2000*. Have students then develop a cluster with *Write Source 2000* as the nucleus word. (See 035 in the handbook for an explanation of clustering.) Or, have them write freely for 5 or 10 minutes (the focus of this writing should be their first impressions). Discuss the results of their clustering or writing.
- Have students develop who, what, when, where, why, and how questions from *Write Source 2000*. Students should then exchange questions with a partner and search for answers in the handbook. Upon completion, partners should share their answers.

  Example questions:

  Who would make an interesting figure for a character sketch?

  What is the first step in the writing process?

Special Challenge: Develop questions that teams of students try to answer using the handbook. Pattern this activity after a popular game show.

Using Write Source 2000

Your First Week with the Handbook

DAY 1 ■ Duplicate and distribute "You Have Been Called!" Have your students work on this activity on their own or in pairs. Help students with the first question on this sheet.

DAY 2 ■ Provide time at the beginning of the class period for students to complete their handbook planning. When they complete this activity, have students share their design ideas.

Pass out individual copies of *Write Source 2000*. Give students sufficient time to review their handbooks. For an assignment, have students complete the activity sheet "Compare and Contrast."

DAY 3 ■ Discuss the comparisons between the handbooks the students have designed and *Write Source 2000*.

Review "Using the Handbook" page in the handbook. Have students practice using *Write Source 2000* with a Scavenger Hunt activity. Have them complete this activity for the next day.

DAY 4 ■ Discuss the completed Scavenger Hunt. (Note the answer key on this page for the prepared activity sheets.)

Then have students find a page, a short section, a set of guidelines, an illustration, etc., that they find interesting or entertaining. Students should prepare to share their discoveries on the next day.

DAY 5 ■ Students should present their "finds" in discussion groups or as a class. With any time remaining, select one of the Scavenger Hunt activities (preferably "Easy Liftoff") to implement.

ANSWER KEY

Scavenger Hunt A (page 15)

1. 13° N, 122° E (See 831 or 833.)
2. flock or gaggle (See 797.)
3. time (See 378.)
4. Students can choose from *buzz, gunk, gushy, swish, zigzag, zing,* or *zip.* (See 232.)
5. Reword the test question into a topic sentence. (See 424.)
6. Be realistic about the goals you set. (See 451.)
7. a page at the end of a report that lists in alphabetical order the books and materials you have used in your report (See 281, 283.)
8. Reserve a section of a notebook for each class you would like to write about. (See 410.)
9. list of all the latest magazine articles (See 299.)
10. independent clauses that are not connected with a coordinate conjunction (or) independent clauses when the clauses are connected only by a conjunctive adverb (See 484.)
11. inside (See 515.)
12. 2,204.6 pounds (See 803.)

Scavenger Hunt B (page 16)

1. selecting/collecting/connecting/correcting (See 012.)
2. Take inventory of people you know or have heard about. (See 155.)
3. The heading includes the sender's complete address and the full date. (See 205.)
4. recalling information (See 312.)
5. together or with (See 374.)
6. a word used in place of a noun (See 733.)
7. "imaginary gardens with real toads in them" (See 221.)
8. either, or; neither, nor; not only, but also; both, and; whether, or (See 792 for more.)
9. these words are used as names (See 542.)
10. you can divide a word at the end of a line (See 303.)

Easy Liftoff (page 18)

1. 458
2. personal writing (129-149)
3. 366
4. 14 (See 234.)
5. 176
6. hypn (See 380.)
7. right of trial by jury (See 874.)
8. had been found (See 759 chart.)
9. Krakow (See 840.)
10. 350-355

Getting Started Scenario

What Would You Put in a Handbook?

- **The scenario you are about to read challenges you to solve a problem—what would you put in a student handbook?**

You Have Been Called!

You have been called to New York by Mrs. McGuffey, a famous and successful editor of an equally famous and respected educational publishing company. When you are escorted into her office, she surprises you by asking, "What would you put in a student handbook if you wanted students, like you, to really use it? I want to publish a handbook so powerful that students will take it to all their classes and then take it home to help them with their homework. That's why I've asked you to come to New York. Will you help me design this handbook?"

What would you put in a student handbook?

What would it look like? What title would you give it?

What would you do to make it easy to use?

Why do you think students would like and use the handbook you have planned?

(Use the space below to start your planning.)

The cover of my book will look like this:

Getting Started Scenario

What Would You Put in a Handbook?

■ **When you have completed your plan, review your copy of *Write Source 2000*. Compare the handbook with the one you have designed.**

Compare and Contrast

Is the handbook you designed like ours? Does *Write Source 2000* have some of the same information you chose to put in the handbook you designed? What different information does your handbook contain?

Same Information	Different Information

Does *Write Source 2000* look like the handbook you designed?

Same Appearance	Different Appearance

Getting to Know the Write Source 2000 *Handbook*

Scavenger Hunt A

If you have not already learned how to use the handbook, read "Using the Handbook" at the front of *Write Source 2000*. Once you understand how your handbook works, use it to answer the questions that follow.

1. Using the maps in your *Write Source 2000*, identify the lines of **latitude** and **longitude** (in degrees) for the Philippines. ________________ and ________________

2. A group of **geese** is called a ________________________________.

3. The **root** *chron* means ________________________________.

4. Three examples of **onomatopoeia** are ________________________, ________________________, and ________________________.

5. What is the main idea of the **minilesson** in "Planning and Writing the Essay Answer"?

   ____

   ____

6. Identify the first guideline for **setting a goal.** ________________________________

   ____

7. A **bibliography** is ____

   ____.

8. What is the first step you would take if you wanted to start a **learning log?** ____________

   ____

   ____

9. The *Readers' Guide* is an organized ________________________________.

10. A **semicolon** is used to join two ________________________________

    ____.

11. Periods and commas are placed ________________________ **quotation marks.**

12. How many pounds in one **metric** ton? ________________________________

Getting to Know the Write Source 2000 *Handbook*

Scavenger Hunt B

If you have not already learned how to use the handbook, read "Using the Handbook" at the front of *Write Source 2000*. Once you understand how your handbook works, use it to answer the questions that follow.

1. Identify the four steps in the **writing process.**

 ____

2. Identify the first "selecting" guideline in "**Writing Phase Biographies.**"

 ____

 ____

3. List the information found in a heading for a **business letter.**

 ____

4. Identify the most basic **level of thinking** you practice in school.

 ____

5. The **prefix** "co" means ____.

6. A **pronoun** is ____

 ____.

7. What is Marianne Moore's definition of **poetry?** ____

 ____

8. List three pairs of **correlative conjunctions.** ____

 ____

9. Capitalize words such as *mother, father, aunt,* and *uncle* when ____

 ____.

10. The **dictionary** is often used to determine where ____

 ____.

Getting to Know My Handbook

Find suitable words to complete the chart below. Be sure the words you select begin with the letters in the left-hand column. Use each word only once. *Note:* You may not find a word that corresponds to each letter for all of the categories.

	Commonly Misspelled Words	Thinking Terms (See 330)	Computer Terms	Prepositions	Commonly Mixed Pairs (See 574)	Countries I Have Never Seen	Topics I Would Like to Write About
W	weird						
R							
I							
T							
E							
S							
O							
U							
R							
C							
E							

Getting to Know
The *Write Source 2000* Handbook

Easy Liftoff

■ **Do these simple warm-ups and you'll be flying through *Write Source 2000* in no time.**

1. *(Preposterously easy)* Using the table of contents, find the topic number where "The Yellow Pages" begin. ____________

2. *(Ridiculously easy)* Using the table of contents again, find out which major unit contains sections on writing about personal experiences. ____________

3. *(Piece of cake)* Using the index of topics at the back of the book, find the topic number where you would learn about SQ3R. ____________

4. *(Pretty simple)* Starting in the index, find out how many lines are in a Shakespearean sonnet. ____________

5. *(No sweat)* Find the topic number for the sample news story. ____________

6. *(Easier than you think)* What is the root for the word "hypnosis"? ____________

7. *(Not too hard)* What is the topic of Amendment 7 to the Constitution of the United States?

   ____

8. *(Could be worse)* What is the past perfect passive form of the verb "find"?

   ____

9. *(OK, this is a challenge, but you can do it.)* What European city is located at 20° east longitude and 50° north latitude?

   ____

10. *(If you can answer this, you're airborne!)* Find the topic numbers where examples of "fuzzy thinking" are given.

    ____

Using Write Source 2000:
Long-Range Activities

Periodically select pages, guidelines, checklists, or models for your students to read and react to in discussion groups or as a class. Instruct students to take note of information they find new, interesting, and helpful with a small check (✓) and information they have questions about with a small question mark (?). The information that is checked or questioned becomes the focus of their discussion. (Students should make their marks in pencil, so they can erase them later on.)

On a regular basis conduct minilessons that give your students practice using *Write Source 2000*. (Sample minilessons follow; additional minilessons can be found on pages 133-152.)

I'm stuck, I'm stuck. .... *Breaking Writer's Block*

■ The only sure cure for writer's block is writing anyway. You've got to get back to the start, where you don't give a hoot, where writing is just a fling. To get there,

READ topic numbers **004** and **005**, "An Invitation to Writing."

DO exactly what you're told in **005**, "Preparing for Liftoff." When you're done, you won't be preparing anymore. You'll be off!

Me-Maps .... *Creating a "SourceBank"*

■ To build up ideas to write about, read the paragraph on the "Life Map" (**034**).

TRY a different kind of "Me-Map" like one of these:

- A "Cut Map"—my best and worst cuts and scrapes
- A "Sandwich Map"—my best and worst sandwiches
- A "Talk Map"—how I learned to talk
- A "Fall Map"—my best and worst trips, plunges, spills, and collapses
- A "Dare Map"—the best and worst chances I've taken

INVENT a "Me-Map" of your own.

In, Under, and Around .... *Using Prepositions*

■ Review the rules for using prepositions in "The Yellow Pages" (**788-790**).

COMPOSE a poem of at least five lines, on any subject, in which each line begins with a different preposition. (See **236** for a model.) **SHARE** finished products.

Using *Write Source 2000* in the Classroom

Where does *Write Source 2000* fit in?

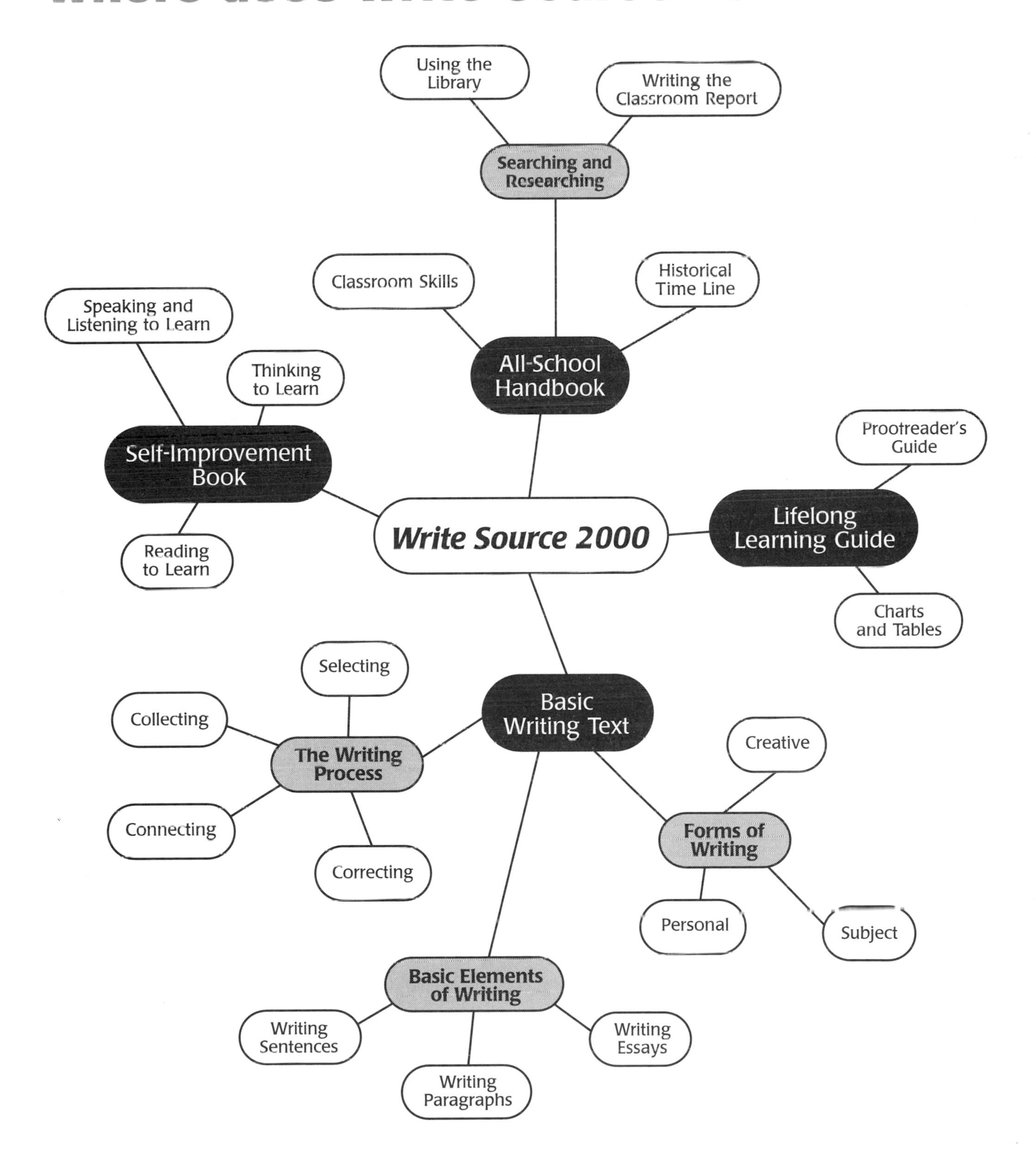

Using the Library
Writing the Classroom Report
Searching and Researching
Classroom Skills
Historical Time Line
Speaking and Listening to Learn
Thinking to Learn
All-School Handbook
Self-Improvement Book
Proofreader's Guide
Write Source 2000
Lifelong Learning Guide
Reading to Learn
Charts and Tables
Selecting
Collecting
The Writing Process
Basic Writing Text
Creative
Connecting
Correcting
Forms of Writing
Personal
Subject
Basic Elements of Writing
Writing Sentences
Writing Essays
Writing Paragraphs

Building a Writing and Language Program with the *Write Source 2000* Handbook

Q. Can teachers build a language program with *Write Source 2000* and the *Teacher's Guide*?

A. Most definitely. These two resources can serve as the foundation for a contemporary language arts program promoting, among other things, student-centered language learning, writing as a process of discovery, and the reading-writing connection. These products can also serve as the foundation for a cross-curricular writing and learning program.

Q. How should teachers plan a program with these two resources?

A. Since *Write Source 2000* functions mainly as a writing handbook, that is where teachers should first focus their attention. Two very basic questions should be answered during initial planning: **How will writing instruction be approached?** (Will students engage in writing workshops? Will writing be integrated into thematic units?) **What types of writing will be covered?** (Will personal forms of writing be emphasized in grade 6? Will paragraphs be of primary importance in grades 6 and 7 and multiparagraph essays in grade 8?)

"Contemporary Writing Programs," pages 59-61 in the *Teacher's Guide*, will help teachers answer the first question. All of the important approaches to writing instruction are discussed here. Teachers can answer the second question by reviewing the forms of writing covered in the handbook and focusing their attention on those forms that best meet the needs and nature of their students. (Teachers may also refer to the framework of writing activities for grades 6-8 listed on page 25 in this section for a suggested sequence of writing activities.)

Q. What about the other language arts?

A. Teachers will find major sections in the handbook related to reading, thinking, and speaking and listening.

Reading to Learn (360-387) • We suggest that a number of different study-reading strategies be practiced at each grade level. We also suggest that the glossary of prefixes, suffixes, and roots be the focus of vocabulary study.

Thinking to Learn (305-359) • This section addresses thinking from a number of different perspectives. The primary focus of attention in one grade level might be clear and logical thinking, in another grade level, creative thinking, and so on.

Speaking and Listening to Learn (388-407) • The basic guidelines included in this section should be used year after year.

Q. What about learning and study skills?

A. In the handbook's "Learning to Learn" section (408-457), teachers will find a variety of guidelines related to studying and learning. Perhaps writing to learn and note taking could be emphasized in one grade level, test taking in the next grade, and individual skills (setting goals, managing time, etc.) in the following grade.

Q. What else should teachers remember when planning with *Write Source 2000*?

A. Teachers should always remember to turn to the "Section by Section Teacher's Notes" in the *Teacher's Guide* (pages 29-55) whenever they are planning a unit around a particular section or chapter in the handbook.

Important: A SourceBook of writing and learning activities is available for each grade—6, 7, and 8. (See pages 156-161 for more.)

What specific types of writing are covered in *Write Source 2000*?

The chart below lists many of the types of writing discussed in the *Write Source 2000* handbook. The types of writing are listed in this manner to indicate a possible framework or sequence of activities, moving from personal writing to writing that eventually becomes more inventive and reflective. Teachers can use this framework as a starting point when planning a writing program (or individual writing activities) with the handbook.

	6	7	8
PERSONAL WRITING			
Recording	Writing to Learn (004) Journal Writing (130)	Creating a SourceBank (033) Journal Writing (132)	Learning Logs (409) Journal Writing (132)
Recalling and Remembering	Writing About Experiences (144) Memories of People (149)	Writing About Experiences (144) Memories of Places (149)	Writing Phase Autobiographies (133) Memories of Objects (149)
SUBJECT WRITING			
Introducing	Bio-Poems (158)	The Character Sketch (159)	Writing Phase Biographies (151)
Describing	Descriptive Paragraphs (077) Describing a Person (068)	Descriptive Paragraphs (077) Describing a Place (069)	Describing an Object (070) Describing an Event (072)
Reporting	Writing the Basic News Story (171)	Writing the Feature Story (177)	Writing a News Story (171)
Corresponding	Writing Friendly Letters (196)	Writing Fan Letters (192)	Writing Business Letters (203)
Informing	Narrative Paragraphs (078) Expository Paragraphs (079)	Narrative Paragraphs (078) Expository Paragraphs (079)	Multiparagraph Essays (052) Expository Paragraphs (079)
Searching and Researching	Writing Summaries (184) Library Report (271, 290)	Writing Summaries (184) Report Writing (271)	Writing Summaries (184) Personal Research Paper (265)
CREATIVE WRITING			
Translating	"Invented" Poetry (235)	Free-Verse Poetry (224)	Traditional Poetry (233)
Inventing	Story Writing (237) Writing Mystery Stories (248)	Story Writing (237) Writing Myths (251)	Story Writing (237) Patterned Stories (246)
Scripting	Dialogue Writing (253)	Monologue Writing (253, 245)	Writing Miniplays (257)
REFLECTIVE WRITING			
Analyzing and Classifying	Writing a Comparison and Contrast Essay (064)	Writing About Problems and Solutions (066)	Cause and Effect Writing (066) Writing to Define (071)
Persuading	Persuasive Paragraphs (080)	Writing Pet Peeves (050)	Writing Editorials (178, 074)
Reviewing	One-Paragraph Book Reviews (187)	One-Paragraph Book Reviews (187)	Multiparagraph Book Reviews (187)

What additional topics are covered in *Write Source 2000?*

There is an incredible amount of information covered in *Write Source 2000*, a good deal of which goes unnoticed (or unmentioned) in a quick review of the handbook's key features. What follows is a list of information teachers will discover once they carefully read through *Write Source 2000*. This list further demonstrates the handbook's potential as a teaching and learning tool.

Note: Refer to pages 133-152 for minilessons related to many of these writing, learning, and cross-curricular topics.

Writing-Related Topics

- Creating a Writing "SourceBank" (033-034)
- Selecting a Writing Subject (035-036)
- Writing Prompts, Topics, and Forms (039-041)
- Organizing with an Outline (059-062)
- Transition or Linking Words (089)
- Improving Your Style of Writing (116-117)
- Writing Techinques and Terms (124-128)
- Writing Fan Letters (192-195)
- Computers & Writing (287-289)
- Avoiding Fuzzy Thinking in Writing (350-355)
- Handwriting Models (911)

Language and Learning Topics

- Reading and Understanding Your Book (187)
- What Is Poetry? (221-223)
- Reading and Appreciating a Poem (229)
- An Introduction to Traditional Poetry (230-234)
- Basic Patterns for Stories (246)
- Using the Library (290-304)
- Becoming a Better Thinker (307)
- Using Your Brain (356-359)
- Word Pictures for Reading to Learn (365)
- Using Context Clues (370)
- Completing Assignments (453)
- Managing Stress (455-457)
- Improved Spelling (568-573)
- Reading Charts (811-825)

Cross-Curricular Topics in "The Student Almanac"

- Animal Facts (797)
- Braille Alphabet and Numbers (799)
- Tables of Weights and Measures (803-808)
- Planet Profusion (809)
- Periodic Table of the Elements (810)
- Improving Math Skills (843-855)
- Using the Computer (856-864)
- All About Maps (826-842)
- Historical Documents (865-888)
- Historical Time Line (889-898)

How can *Write Source 2000* meet the needs of every student?

> *"The education of young people, including their language, is different for every place, for every school, for every class, and—most importantly—for every person."*
>
> —RUTH CLINE AND ROBERT C. SMALL, JR.

Teachers can't possibly accommodate all of their students' different learning styles following a standard text, one chapter after another. What works best is a language resource like *Write Source 2000*, providing useful information and guidelines that each student can turn to on his or her own terms.

All middle-level students will find helpful information, guidelines, and examples in the handbook. We like to call *Write Source 2000* a con-textbook because students refer to it when they have a need for information. Basic paragraphs, letters, reports, poems, stories, study skills, proofreading—it's all in *Write Source 2000.* This one book truly does "fit all sizes."

Reform and Restructuring

Today, many educators are shifting more and more of their attention to helping students explore their own interests and improve their emerging abilities. Instead of the assembly-line approach to teaching with the products being the students (having survived the system), students are being addressed on their own terms, with their individual needs at the core of the curriculum. "Instead of teachers teaching subjects, they are teaching students" (Cline and Small).

Student-Centered Learning

Certainly, this way of thinking has affected language instruction more than any other area of the curriculum. For what could be more student centered than writing and reading workshops? Workshops evolve around the students' learning. They write at their own pace, read books that interest them, interact, take risks, decide what projects to work on next, and so on.

So what does *Write Source 2000* have to do with a discussion of workshops? Well, we've used the workshop approach in our own classrooms, so we know how effective it can be. Former students tell us all the time how they really learned to write and read in our language arts classes. It's also because of the workshop approach that we developed our first handbook. We did it to give our students a basic resource they could refer to when writing, reading, and learning. A book like *Write Source 2000* can be the glue that helps hold a workshop together.

Meeting Everyone's Needs

Once your students have their own copies of *Write Source 2000*, we can't urge you enough to turn your classroom into a workshop. It is the best way, really the only way, to meet your students' individual needs. Everyone reads, writes, and learns together. When workshops are used effectively, grouping or tracking isn't necessary.

Making It Work

Workshop teachers must become effective managers of their classrooms, providing an atmosphere conducive to writing and learning. And they must guide students and help them master basic skills during personal conferences, during group editing sessions, and in occasional whole-class periods of instruction.

Read *In the Middle* by Nancie Atwell and *Seeking Diversity* by Linda Rief for two thorough discussions about the operation and successful management of writing and reading workshops. Both books are available from Heinemann-Boynton/Cook Publishers. Also see pages 67-68 in this guide for additional information on workshops.

Section by Section

Teacher's Notes

The following pages contain a section by section overview of *Write Source 2000* with specific suggestions and helpful hints for using the handbook in your classroom.

Write Source 2000

Section by Section Teacher's Notes

Writing to Learn

Rationale: We realize how many students approach writing. They begin each writing project with one idea in mind—completing it. They aim straight for the finish line and bypass all of the interesting twists and turns each project has to offer. All of their energy goes into producing something to turn in, something as free of careless errors as they can make it, and, unfortunately, something that falls far short of what they are capable of producing.

Our purpose in "Writing to Learn" is to direct your students' enthusiasm and energy in the right direction, so they can produce writing that they feel good about and you and your students can enjoy reading. (We were teachers ourselves, so we know it's no picnic reading a set of "who can get to the finish line first" pieces of writing.)

Chapter Summaries

004-010 Writing to Learn

Students need to know that writing is much more than just another assignment. They need to see writing not only as an effective learning tool, but also as an important part of a satisfying life—right up there with exercise and a well-balanced diet. That's our purpose in this short chapter—to help students appreciate what writing has to offer them.

We identify six different types of learning that can be enhanced by putting pen to paper. By writing, students can better learn about themselves, their immediate world, their acquaintances, LIFE (as in the big picture), their course work, and their initial ideas for writing assignments.

If your students are reluctant writers, try this one on them: Tell them that if they write regularly in and out of school, they will get better grades. They won't necessarily turn into straight-A students, but they can't help but improve their grades if they follow our advice for personal and school-related writing in this chapter as well as throughout the handbook.

Getting Started: To help students experience writing as a personal learning tool, we open with "An Invitation to Writing." Have students "lift off" into writing with this activity before you read and discuss the rest of the chapter.

Enrichment: If you want your students to begin writing in a personal journal after reading and discussing "Writing to Learn," see "Keeping a Personal Journal" (130) in the handbook.

011-027 The Writing Process

No one—not even the most accomplished writer—gets his or her writing right the first time. Writing must go through a process or series of steps before it's ready to share with readers. Your challenge—and the challenge of all teachers who have their students write—is to make sure that your students appreciate this fact as well. "The Writing Process" is designed to help you meet this challenge.

"Writing in Action" (011), the introduction to "The Writing Process," describes for your students how professional writers develop a piece of writing. What follows is an explanation of the steps in the writing process and how your students can make use of these steps when they develop their own writing.

Getting Started: Before you read and discuss any part of "The Writing Process," have your students describe their personal "process" of writing—that is, the way in which they have generally completed writing assignments in the past. Compare this process to the one described in this chapter. Later in the quarter, have students describe how their personal process of writing has changed after working with *Write Source 2000* for a few of their writing projects.

Special Points of Interest:

012 "The Steps in the Process" (These steps serve as the focus for all of the forms of writing discussed in *Write Source 2000.*)

017 "Focusing Your Efforts" (Students must understand that they don't have to say everything in their writing.)

021 "Connecting: Revising Your Writing" (What student doesn't need help and advice with revising?)

027 "Correcting and Proofreading Checklist" (Students should always refer to this checklist when they are putting the finishing touches on their writing.)

Enrichment: Have students in pairs list at least four or five important things they remember to do when they write.

■ Here are some things we feel are important for you and your students to remember about writing. (You might want to refer to our ideas during the discussion of your students' lists.)

- ☐ Writing should be approached as a process of discovery, not as an end product.
- ☐ Writers should write about something that interests them.
- ☐ Writers should be knowledgeable about the subject of their writing.
- ☐ Writers should share their work throughout the writing process.
- ☐ Writers should write for an intended audience, even if that means their fellow writers.
- ☐ Writers should write in an honest and sincere voice.

Post a list of "Keys to Good Writing" in your classroom where all of your students can see it. And remind students to refer to this list whenever they are developing a piece of writing. (Make changes in the list as the year progresses.)

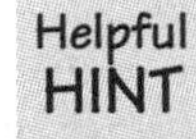

Make sure that your students understand that a writer does not progress in a linear fashion through the steps in the writing process. There is a lot of forward and backward motion. As writing researcher Sandra Perl states, "People go back to the words on the page in order to move forward."

> "Sharing allows writers to hear what their ideas sound like and to solicit feedback as they continue to think about a topic, draft, or revise."
>
> —KAREN SPEAR

028-029 Group Advising

Writers need to talk about their writing with fellow writers. That's why writing groups are so important. They promote a writing community in your classroom, and they promote the give-and-take of writing ideas that will help your students grow as writers. "Group Advising" provides you and your students with guidelines for conducting productive sharing sessions.

Getting Started: Have students write freely for 10 minutes about anything they wish. (Refer them to 039-041 for writing ideas.) Then have them share their free writing with a classmate using the "Writing Group Guidelines" (028). Instruct listeners to make at least one positive comment and ask at least two questions that would help the writers develop their writing.

Where do you go from here? Have students work their initial free writings into finished pieces (with the help of the handbook and their classmates in group advising sessions). Or have them move on to another type of writing for additional group practice.

Special Points of Interest:

029 "Commenting on Writing" (Students will find this checklist helpful when they review each other's writing.)

432 "Group Skills" (This chapter provides insights into effective group skills.)

Enrichment: Give your students practice with evaluating writing using the peer editing minilesson on page 86 in this guide.

030-041 Starting Points

"Starting Points" summarizes the steps in the writing process and follows with a number of stimulating prewriting ideas that will help your students search for and shape subjects for almost any type of writing. According to some researchers, at least one third of a student's time during a writing project should be devoted to prewriting and inventing.

Helpful HINT Free writing, listing, and clustering are three effective ways to explore and discover through writing. Give your students plenty of practice using these prewriting techniques.

Getting Started: Use the minilesson "Alphabet Cluster" (page 145 in this guide) to give your students clustering practice. Or, use the minilesson "Twenty-Five Steps" (page 144) to get your students right into free writing.

Enrichment: Early in the year, have your students generate a "SourceBank" of personal writing ideas by developing a "Personal Almanac" or a "Life Map" (034). Provide students with large sheets of paper for their life maps.

THE Basic Elements OF Writing

Rationale: Student writers should make decisions about their work based on the meaning that is evolving in units or large chunks of writing. That is why "The Basic Elements of Writing" opens with discussions of whole compositions—essays and paragraphs—and follows with discussions of sentences.

Chapter Summaries

043-074 Developing Essays

Two general types of essays—the personal essay and the school essay—are discussed in this section. The discussion of the personal essay presents an open-ended look at essay writing—the essay as a catchall personal form of writing. The discussion of the school essay presents a traditional look at essay writing—complete with outlines and thesis statements. This section concludes with guidelines for writing two-part essays (as in comparison and contrast essays) and guidelines for writing essays about people, places, objects, events, and so on.

Getting Started: Before you discuss the guidelines for writing personal essays, have students retrace their actions during part of a typical school day. Tell them that in doing this they are creating a number of possible ideas for a special type of writing. (See 046 for a model. Also take note of the Helpful Hint on that page. You might want to have your students work on this activity instead.)

Where do you go from here? Have your students develop one of their ideas into a personal essay after reviewing with them the guidelines in *Write Source 2000*. Or have them save these ideas in their writing folders for use in the future.

Special Points of Interest:

044 "Writing the Personal Essay" (This form of writing may be new to your students; the school essay will not be.)

058 "Personalizing the School Essay" (Students can add some spark to their school essays with the ideas presented on this page.)

064-074 (These guidelines will help students develop a variety of essay types. Make sure you review them sometime during the first quarter.)

Enrichment: There's nothing like a good gripe session to cleanse the spleen. Have your students sound off with their own pet peeves. (See 050.)

075-089 Building Paragraphs

Everything you and your students need to know about paragraphs (and then some) is included in this section.

Getting Started: Before or during an introductory discussion, have your students think metaphorically about paragraphs and develop "A paragraph is like . . ." statements. For example, a paragraph is like a hamburger—the more you add between the buns, the better it tastes. Or, a paragraph is the middle child of prose, not necessarily as mature as an essay or a whole composition but more developed than an individual sentence. These statements should be shared and made part of a class discussion.

Special Points of Interest:

084 "Methods of Arranging Details" (Students will find this list a handy resource for all of their expository writing.)

087 "Reviewing Paragraphs in Essays, Reports, and Longer Pieces of Writing" (With the guidelines on this page, students can make sure that each of their paragraphs works in longer pieces of writing.)

089 "Transition or Linking Words" (Students will find this chart another handy writing resource.)

Enrichment: Give your students the following challenge: Write a paragraph that includes the following levels of detail: (See 085 in the handbook.)

(1) Controlling (Topic) sentence
  (2) Clarifying sentence
    (3) Completing sentence
    (3) Completing sentence (Optional)
  (2) Clarifying sentence
    (3) Completing sentence
    (3) Completing sentence (Optional)
(1) Controlling (Closing) sentence

Note: This is only a suggested pattern for this paragraph. Adjust it to meet the needs of your students.

090-114 Composing, Combining, and Styling Sentences

When a student writer is ready to edit his or her work, one of the first things to do is check the writing sentence by sentence. He or she should make sure that each sentence expresses a complete thought, that it reads smoothly, and that it is worded in the best possible way. These three chapters on sentences will provide your students with all they need to know when they are reviewing and fine-tuning the sentences in their writing.

Getting Started: Put students into groups of three. Instruct two students to talk about a movie they have both seen, a book they have both read, a game they have both participated in, etc. The third member of the group must listen carefully and record the conversation as it unfolds. (A tape recorder will be a big help for the transcriber.)

Where do you go from here? The transcriptions can be utilized in any number of ways as you read and react to these chapters on sentences. You might, for example, ask each group to volunteer examples of specific sentence errors from their transcriptions when you discuss "Composing Sentences."

Special Points of Interest:

094 "Write 'Agreeable' Sentences" (Remind your students to turn to these pages on common agreement errors whenever they edit their writing.)

102 "Combining Sentences" (This chapter will help students write smoother, more detailed sentences.)

109 "Developing a Sense of Style" (This segment will help students really practice the art of writing.)

Enrichment: Have students keep a file of sentences with style, sentences that are particularly well put in the work of their classmates and from the books and magazines that they read. Encourage students to use these types of sentences in their own writing.

A Special Challenge:

"As a general rule, run your pen through every other word you have written; you have no idea what vigor it will give to your writing style."

—SYDNEY SMITH

Have your students follow Sydney Smith's advice for a recent piece of writing. (They don't, however, have to literally cut every other word.) Then see what they can make of their writing after the cutting.

THE Art OF Writing

Rationale: Professional writers write to discover something new and worthwhile to share with their readers. As writer Donald Murray says, "If the writer does not feel that through writing he will discover something which is uniquely his, he may soon concentrate on craft rather than content." Does this mean that craft is unimportant? Absolutely not. If a writer has something worthwhile to say, he will naturally want to share his ideas as effectively as he can.

Chapter Summaries

116-117 Writing Naturally

Students become writers once they acquire a real feel for writing and develop their natural writing voice. They can best do this by generating a lot of writing—especially the type that is free from the gravitational pull of a teacher's red pen. This is a good reason to get your students writing regularly in a personal journal. Read on in the chapter for more helpful hints.

Getting Started: Have students select a writing prompt (039) to write about freely for 5 to 10 minutes. Have pairs of students exchange papers and make note of sections of their partner's paper that sound especially honest and sincere.

Enrichment: On slips of paper, write *best friend, teacher, parent, uncle, grandmother*, etc. and have students pick one of the slips. Then instruct them to write a friendly letter to this person. You and your students should find that the intended audience affects a writer's natural writing voice. For example, the voice a student uses when writing to a best friend will be different from the voice used when writing to a grandparent.

118-123 Improving Your Writing

Splash, smash, ooze, shriek—all wonderful words, the type of colorful and power-packed words you want your students to use in their writing. The guidelines in "Improving Your Writing" will help your students review their writing for word choice so they include many of the "marvelous English monosyllables."

Getting Started: Have students pantomime strong, colorful words. (See "Pantomime Vocabulary Builder," page 120 in this guide, for guidelines.) You will need a set of thesauruses for this activity.

Enrichment: Have students complete the minilesson "Why We Hiccup" (page 146 in this guide). Remind students that the word choice in each of their explanations should reflect the age and experience of their writing personas.

A Special Challenge: Have your students submit boring paragraphs, paragraphs that hang limp like wet wash. Redistribute the paragraphs so students get new ones. Then have them rewrite these duds using "How do you really know what to change?" (123) as their guide.

124-128 Writing Techniques and Writing Terms

Every possible writing technique and term your students will need to know is listed in these two chapters.

Getting Started: How can you best use this information? Pick and choose those techniques and terms you want your students to know and use. Make a master list for yourself. Then make these words the focus of writing lessons throughout the school year.

Enrichment: Make pairs of students responsible for presenting minilessons on various techniques and terms. For example, you might have one group provide an explanation and examples of parallelism and another group present information on cliches.

Personal Writing

Rationale: "Personal Writing" is the first in a series of three sections that catalog a variety of writing forms.

You and your students can put this information to use in any number of ways. You might use this information to plan a basic writing program by selecting those writing forms you want your students to work with throughout the year. If you conduct a writing workshop, you can rest assured that the information in these sections will provide your students all the help they need with most of their writing projects. And if you're simply looking for guidelines for a certain form of writing, you'll probably find them in one of these three sections.

> *"Advice to young writers? Always the same advice: learn to trust your own judgement, learn inner independence, learn to trust that time will sort the good from the bad."*
>
> —DORIS LESSING

The types of writing in the first two sections progress from very personal types to writing that is gradually more remote, more public in form. The final section describes many creative forms of writing. A lot of our thinking about what forms to include in these sections and in what sequence can be attributed to James Moffett's approach to writing in *Active Voices* (Heinemann-Boynton/Cook, 1981).

Included in "Personal Writing" are guidelines for keeping a personal journal as well as guidelines for writing phase autobiographies and about autobiographical incidents (writing about experiences). Also included are samples of additional forms of personal writing your students might want to work with.

Chapter Summaries

130-132 Journal Writing

We can't think of a more painless and productive way for students to practice writing than doing so in a personal journal. Read and react to 006-010 as well as 130-131 with your students before they begin their journal writing. And make sure that you provide them with the proper send-off for their first journal entry (see 004-005).

Getting Started: Have pairs of students develop a dialogue journal (132) for at least a week. This is an effective beginning-of-the-year activity. Encourage classmates to continue their "conversations" on their own after the week is up.

Enrichment: Have students keep track of their journal writing progress on a chart like the one below.

Date: ______

Topic: ______

Writing Time: ______

Number of Words: ______

Comment: ______

Possible Comments
A. Continue writing on this topic.
B. Continue writing on this topic but from a different angle.
C. Write on a related topic.
D. Write on a topic that unexpectedly developed.
E. Go on to another topic.

133-143 Writing Phase Autobiographies

Most of today's students spend little time reflecting about their past. And small wonder. They are busy enough living life in the present. You can help your students forget about the present for awhile and think about earlier times in their lives by having them write phase autobiographies.

Getting Started: The listing activity (135) provides an easy and effective way for students to recall past experiences. Of course, this activity only becomes important if your students have difficulty thinking of a phase to write about.

Enrichment: Have your students think of their phase autobiographies as just one chapter in their personal stories. Ask them to think of other important chapters in their lives and create a table of contents for their complete autobiographies.

144-149 Writing About Experiences

It's natural and easy for students to talk about their experiences. And it's not hard for them to write about these experiences either. This is one type of writing almost all of my students enjoyed—writing and sharing with their classmates. You'll find writing about experiences to be a perfect activity for early in the year.

Note: This type of writing is known by a number of names, including the autobiographical incident paper and the personal narrative.

Getting Started: Prior to assigning a personal experience paper, have students write a series of journal entries that focus on their experiences. (See 039 in the handbook for writing prompts.) They then have a valuable "SourceBank" of writing ideas to choose from.

Enrichment: Have students praise or bury a memorable object in a brief speech. Let your students' imaginations run wild here. They could prepare a eulogy, an ode, and so on.

Subject Writing

Rationale: Young writers enjoy writing about their own lives and benefit greatly from the experience. But they also need plenty of practice writing about subjects other than themselves. That's why we've developed this extensive section called "Subject Writing." This section provides information on any number of forms of writing, all of which focus on subjects other than the writer. Included are a variety of guidelines from writing phase biographies to writing friendly letters, from writing observation reports to writing book reviews.

Chapter Summaries

151-158 Writing Phase Biographies

A phase biography will take your students beyond their own memories into the lives of relatives, friends, or figures from the past. It offers them a chance to continue the detailing and shaping they learned while writing phase autobiographies. In addition, it offers them a chance to practice interviewing, note taking, and informal researching. Defining a "phase" gives students a chance to practice shaping nonfiction writing to illustrate and support a main idea or focus.

Getting Started: Have your students search for possible writing subjects by free-writing about interesting relatives, ancestors, or acquaintances. Also, have them read and react to "Francis Ann Slocum" (157) as well as to the introductory material (151-154) before they begin developing their phase biographies.

Enrichment: Once your students complete their phase biographies, consider the following activity: Change the point of view of your phase biography so it becomes a phase autobiography—that is, so the subject tells his or her own story. This doesn't mean that your students should completely rewrite their papers. Perhaps they could develop a "phase auto-poem" by adjusting the guidelines for a bio-poem (158) so it reads as if personally written by the subject of the poem.

159-165 Character Sketch

A *phase biography* presents only a significant slice of a person's life. Generally, a *character sketch* presents a subject as he or she is now, in total. (Whatever needs to be explained, described, and shared in a sketch, is . . . so the readers get a good feel for the subject.)

The phase biographer asks himself, "How can I best share with my readers an important time in my subject's life?" While the writer of a character sketch asks himself, "How can I effectively share the 'big picture' of who this person is?"

The phase biographer starts with a certain framework already in place—a period of time in the subject's life. The writer of a character sketch has no such framework. He must pick and choose from the facts and details he has gathered and establish his own parameters.

Getting Started: The minilesson "Eyes Like Meteors" (see page 147 in this guide) provides an effective starting point for this project.

Enrichment: Explain the guidelines for this activity a day ahead of time, so students can prepare pantomimes to go along with their character sketches.

Ask students to select a passage, an incident, a characteristic action, etc., from their sketches to pantomime. When called upon, they should perform their pantomimes. After each, instruct the audience to briefly describe what they observed.

166-170 Observation Report

After they write about personal experiences and the experiences of others, have your students look beyond "people-types" and focus their attention on a particular place in an observation report.

Getting Started: An observation report without good sensory detail is like an oatmeal raisin cookie without the raisins. One of the most important ingredients is missing.

You'll need to do whatever you can to help your students focus on sensory details. One thing you can do is have your students study the sensory detail used in the model observation report (170). You might also try this activity.

Have your students show proper respect for their own senses by listing their most enjoyable sensations: (Encourage them to list as many sensations as they can.)

- ☐ Scent-sation (Identify the smells you like.) Example: Just-baked bread
- ☐ Touch-able (Identify things you like to touch.) Example: Freshly poured cement
- ☐ Taste-ful (Identify the tastes you like.) Example: A tart apple
- ☐ Sight-ly (Identify the sights you like.) Example: Your weekly allowance
- ☐ Sound-er (Identify the sounds you like.) Example: The 3:00 dismissal bell

Enrichment: Instruct your students to look very closely at one of their fingernails. Tell them that the fingernail is a window to another world. Have them write an observation report on what they see.

> *"Good writing is filled with specific, accurate, honest information. The reader is persuaded through authoritative information that the writer knows the subject."*
>
> —DONALD MURRAY

171-177 Writing the News Story

It seemed like detective Joe Friday in the old *Dragnet* television series was forever saying something like "just the facts, ma'am" to witnesses and suspects he interviewed during investigations. It's "just the facts" that you will want your students to emphasize in their newswriting. And you will want them to use these facts in a special way as outlined in this chapter on writing the news story.

Getting Started: Give your students newswriting practice by having them write a brief, but complete news article about a memorable event in their lives. Also, make sure that you review the writing guidelines and the model story with your students before they start out.

Enrichment: Have groups of students plan and present "Live at 5 (or 8 or 9)" news broadcasts or telecasts.

178-183 Writing an Editorial

There's probably no skill more difficult for young writers to grasp than developing a persuasive argument. They need as much practice with persuasive writing as you can give them. "Writing an Editorial" is an effective, practical, and productive method of persuasive writing for your students to work with. It's especially productive if your school publishes its own newspaper.

Getting Started: If your students have trouble selecting a subject suitable for an editorial, try the following activity: Have your students (on their own or in pairs) make a list of "What would happen if . . .?" statements: "What would happen if the only theater in town closed?" "What would happen if the computer lab were open during the lunch hour?" "What would happen if students had to pass a competency (ability) test?" One of these statements might serve as a starting point for an effective editorial.

Helpful HINT Before students develop their own editorials, share a number of models with them. (See 183 and 213 for two examples.) Evaluate these models using the handbook as a guide (182).

Enrichment: Have your students break every rule in the book in a "fractured editorial."

Encourage them to assume a new persona for their editorials. On the day that their work is shared, suggest that they dress and act the part of their persona.

If students need rules to break, have them refer to "Fuzzy Thinking," 350, as well as to the regular guidelines in this chapter.

184-186 Writing a Summary

Why should students write summaries? For two basic reasons. They can write summaries to help themselves make sense out of new concepts and materials presented in their classes. In this way, summary writing is an effective writing-to-learn technique. They can also write summaries to indicate to you what they have learned. This is writing to show what they have learned.

As a writing-to-learn technique, students should write summaries as they "think"—in language that is personal, informal, and colloquial. And obviously, when students write summaries to show what they have learned, they should develop their thoughts according to the guidelines established for the assignment or task. As with any form of writing, students can only acquire a real feel for summarizing through regular practice.

Getting Started: After you've discussed the guidelines for summary writing with your students, read aloud "An Invitation to Learning" (001). Instruct students to follow along carefully and, perhaps, list a few main ideas. Then have them review the reading on their own and write a brief summary of this section. Follow with a general discussion of their summaries.

Enrichment: Have pairs of students practice summarizing in the following way: Have each team select a form of writing in *Write Source 2000* to read and learn about. (A page or two of information at a time will do.)

One member reads while the other member becomes an active listener. The listener tells what he or she has heard after the reading. The team then decides together what the essential information is in the reading. Both the reader and listener should write a brief paragraph summarizing what they have learned. These can be compared as well.

187-191 The Book Review

An opening word of caution: When you assign book reviews, you are essentially asking your students to evaluate the books they have read. Evaluating is a very advanced level of thinking and writing, and it is not easily mastered. (See 330 for a chart of the different levels of thinking and writing.) So don't expect convincing reviews from young writers. They are only learning to appreciate literature and write about it.

Getting Started: Students really need to become personally engaged in the books they read if you're going to have them write book reviews. That is, they need to explore their personal thoughts and feelings during their reading, so they have a ready supply of ideas and questions to explore when it comes time to develop their book reviews.

Special Points of Interest:

043 "Developing Essays" (Since a review is basically an essay, these guidelines will help students write their book reviews.)

386 "Elements of Literature" (This list of literary terms will give your students a working vocabulary for their reviews.)

327 "Judging Information" (Students will find this discussion of thinking and writing helpful when they develop their reviews.)

Enrichment: Does a book review have to look like your basic essay? We don't think so. We recommend that you give your students a variety of ways to review the books they have read. You might have your students

- ☐ create bookmarks or posters for the books they read, as if they were a marketing agent trying to sell the book,
- ☐ write thoughtful letters about the book to the author,
- ☐ present their thinking about the book to the class (perhaps an oral reading could be worked into their presentation), or
- ☐ participate in panel discussions about the books that they read.

192-219 Writing Letters

Students need to write to people outside of the classroom for real reasons. And why? They take their writing more seriously if they know someone "out there" is going to read what they have to say. Letter writing is tailor-made for this purpose—especially business letter writing. This section includes guidelines and models for writing business letters. You will also find guidelines for writing friendly letters.

Getting Started: You might want to ask your students to react to the following question: How important is letter writing to you? Consider reading the introductory page on letter writing in *Write Source 2000* (192) before or after you ask this question.

You might also have students brainstorm for situations when a letter would be the best way to communicate. Or you might have them do a little personal research about letter writing. Have them talk to friends, immediate family members, and relatives about letter writing.

Enrichment: (For a business letter) Have students write a "fan" letter along the lines of the model in *Write Source 2000*. (See 195.)

Rationale: Creative thinking and writing don't automatically happen as soon as you ask your students to write a poem, a story, or a short play. Creativity is much too temperamental for that. Students must be stimulated and challenged before they will put their imaginations to work. They must be encouraged to take risks and know that it is okay to make mistakes. And they must have your support as they develop their work.

It's up to you to make sure that these conditions are met so that creativity feels welcome in your classroom. Then it's up to your students to shape their creative thinking and writing into effective finished pieces.

> *"Clearly, by the 'creative process,' we mean the capacity to find new and unexpected dimensions, to voyage freely over the seas, to happen on America as we seek new routes to India, to find new relationships in time and space, and thus new meanings."*
>
> —LAWRENCE S. KUBIE

Chapter Summaries

221-236 Writing Poetry

Students only need to give poetry a chance, and they'll find it an enjoyable form of writing to work with—if for no other reason than that it's a change from the type of writing they normally do. The key is to make poetry appealing, nonthreatening, and fun . . . right from the start.

Getting Started: Have your students produce a poem right away. Once they realize that they are, in fact, poets in the making, they'll be much more receptive to reading about poetry in their handbooks and writing additional poems.

Here's an easy and almost foolproof way your students can produce an effective little poem. Have them take a close look at your school and record three or four brief scenes that draw their attention. (Tell them to look for things that would make for interesting snapshots.) Have your students write one sentence for each observation.

Next, have your students pull the rug from under one or more of their sentences so that the words spill into a tumble-down poem as in the example that follows:

Sentence: These dusty stairs lead to the attic room where old, forgotten band uniforms lay.

Tumble-Down Poem: These dusty stairs
lead to the attic room
where
old, forgotten
band uniforms
lay.

Special Points of Interest:

229 "Reading and Appreciating a Poem" (Take time to read and appreciate a wide variety of poems with your students. The guidelines on this page will help you and your students get the most out of the poems you read.)

230 "An Introduction to Traditional Poetry" (Anything your students will need to know about traditional poetry is included here.)

235 "The Forms of 'Invented' Poetry" (Give your students every opportunity to experiment with a number of these forms.)

Enrichment: Here's another poetic form you might want to try with your students: Have them preserve some of their random thoughts in a **thought-trap poem**. First, have students identify some object (a book, a purse, a doodle on a folder, etc.) in the first line of their poems. Then ask students to list random thoughts as they come to mind. Encourage them to list ideas nonstop until they feel it is time to trap these thoughts in a poem by repeating the first line.

237-252 Story Writing

In the first line of "Story Writing" we remind your students that each one of them is a born storyteller. And we really believe that. We vividly remember all of the students in our own classes who loved to tell stories about their personal experiences. Storytelling was natural, enjoyable, and necessary for them—it reaffirmed their special place among their classmates.

> *"Whatever you write, no matter how abstract or impersonal it might be, you are always telling some part of your own story. It's impossible to put pen to paper without revealing something about yourself."*
>
> —JOHN ROUSE

We also recognize that the personal stories students are so willing to share serve as a perfect lead into writing fiction. How so? Much of fiction stems from true stories that have simply been rerouted in some way from their original courses. Names may have been changed, incidents may have been altered, conflicts may have been added—but essentially many of the stories your students read are based on real-life situations. This is an important point to keep in mind. Your students already have plenty of raw material to draw from as they begin to write fiction. They just need practice "reshaping" their own stories into effective finished pieces. The guidelines in "Story Writing" will help them meet this end.

Getting Started: Have students in pairs share surprising, amusing, and important personal experiences. Afterward, ask for volunteers to share their stories with the class. Select one of the stories to analyze. That is, as a class, identify the main parts of the story: the characters, the setting, the main activity, and the conflict. Have students do the same for one of their own stories. Then, help students fictionalize their stories by altering one or more of the main parts.

Where do you go from here? After reviewing the guidelines for story writing in the handbook, why not have students develop their altered personal stories into pieces of fiction?

Special Points of Interest:

239 "Inventing Stories: A How-to Interview with a Real Story Writer" (This interview provides plenty of practical advice plus plenty of laughs.)

244 "Connecting: Taking Inventory of Your Story" (This checklist will help your students evaluate their work in progress.)

253 "Writing Dialogue" (Stories need dialogue. This chapter answers any questions students may have about writing dialogue.)

Enrichment: Have your students individually or in pairs plan a popular short story. Suggest that students choose from the story types described in the short story sampler (247). A simple plan for students to follow is provided in the interview in this chapter (see 239).

253-256 Writing Dialogue

What language arts teacher isn't frustrated by the way many students use or misuse dialogue in their writing? Either it sounds too stiff and unnatural, it ends too abruptly or continues on much too long, or it is "punctuated" in a way that makes it almost impossible to follow. "Writing Dialogue" won't remake your students into skilled writers of discourse; only plenty of practice and guidance will do that. But this brief chapter does provide plenty of practical advice that will at least point your student writers in the right direction.

Getting Started: Have your students complete "Road Trip," a minilesson on writing dialogue on page 149 in this guide. (See the section on minilessons.)

Note: Make sure you share examples of effectively written dialogue and discuss this chapter before students work on this minilesson.

Enrichment: Review "Imaginary Conversations" (254) with your class. Then have them develop imaginary conversations of their own. They can use the prompt given in the handbook or come up with one of their own. Remind them to refer to "The Yellow Pages" for help with punctuating.

257-263 Writing Plays

A story is a story—whether it is played out in narrative form or "acted out" by a set of interesting characters in a play. As a result, the way you and your students approach play or script writing should not be a great deal different from the way you approach story writing. It's best to begin with the students' own experiences and help them reshape these experiences into basic dramatic forms. We suggest that you begin with basic scripts and move slowly and carefully to more lengthy projects.

If your students have already completed the suggested activities in "Writing Dialogue," they've already worked with very basic script forms. If not, have them work through that brief chapter before tackling "Writing Plays."

". . . plays represent the least abstracted, most detailed rendering of a story possible. Students who have had experience scripting tend, when writing regular narrative, to have a better sense of how much detail is required and when to include or exclude it."

—JAMES MOFFETT AND BETTY JANE WAGNER

Getting Started: Start right in with a "theater in the round" script-writing session: Have your students form into groups of five or six scriptwriters. Then distribute the first few lines of a script to each group. Use the sample script in the handbook (260) if you want, or make up your own.

Then have your students add a line (and perhaps a new character) when the script comes their way. Encourage students to keep the script moving as quickly as possible. When you feel students have had enough, stop the round-robin writing and have one person from each group read their finished product. Students will have fun with this activity. And you might find elements in each of the scripts that deserve to be discussed as you formally introduce "Writing Plays" to your class.

Enrichment: Have students individually or in pairs plan a short play using the "Sample Collection Sheet" (259) as their guide. Encourage your drama freaks to stage their plays.

Searching TO Learn

Rationale: How can you make sure that your students really get engaged in research and report projects? First of all, you must make sure that the entire research process is as lively and active as you can make it. Encourage your students to select research topics that they have a genuine interest in, bring in guest speakers, let your students collaborate on research projects, and so on.

Also, ask your students to gather information from a variety of resources and encourage them to conduct firsthand research. If you establish these general guidelines for your students, they can't help but approach research and report projects with enthusiasm. The guidelines in "Searching to Learn" will help your students put this enthusiasm to good use when they develop personal research papers and classroom reports.

Chapter Summaries

265-270 Personal Research and Writing

What better reason is there for anyone—young learners, teachers, scholars, thoughtful consumers—to engage in research than to answer a pressing question, to satisfy one's curiosity, to basically set out on a personal quest for information? Put another way, what other reason can there be? "Personal Research and Writing" is designed to engage your students in the type of meaningful research just described. We help students select research topics that are of genuine interest to them on a very personal level, we help them conduct their research, and we help them share the results of their work.

Getting Started: If your students have trouble selecting a research subject, have them generate ideas as described in the writing tip (see 268).

You can find any number of personal research projects to use as models in newspapers and magazines. Many feature articles in periodicals tell the story of the writer's quest for information.

Enrichment: After students have carried out a personal research project, challenge them later in the year to develop an engaging personal research story out of a very general subject. Give them a list of topics including apples, cats, flies, stars, cars, trees, and so on, and see what they can make out of one of these.

271-286 The Classroom Report

There's an upside and a downside to assigning reports. First the upside: Reports offer students an opportunity to work with a variety of resources, to compile and organize information, and to develop lengthy pieces of writing.

Now the downside: The starting point for most report assignments is usually a list of teacher-imposed topics, which means students have little freedom to choose a specific subject to research and write about. Also, students often rely on encyclopedias (and other oversized reference books) to compile their reports. Not surprisingly, their finished products resemble the encyclopedia articles they read. And, more often than not, students find it hard to budget their time for an extended project like a report.

Keep these points in mind when your students develop their classroom reports. We feel it's especially important that you encourage your students to write about something that interests them, that they refer to a variety of resources during their research, and that you help them budget their time during the entire research and writing process. Also, make sure that your students refer to "The Classroom Report" for researching and writing advice.

Getting Started: Have students search for possible report topics in the following way: Ask them to do some preliminary research for three possible topics. For each topic, have them identify three interesting things they have learned during their initial research and three different sources they could use to find out more about this topic. From this preliminary research, they can choose a topic for their report.

Special Points of Interest:

280 "Giving Credit for Information Used in a Report" (If you expect your students to give credit in their reports, make sure that you discuss this information with them.)

284 "Model Report" (Encourage students to refer to the model to see firsthand how credit is given in a report and works are cited.)

Enrichment: Have your students put their research and report-writing experience to good use by making your classroom the research and resource center for your school and the community. Have teachers, students, and community members submit questions they want answered, information they want compiled, and references they want checked. Then have students search for answers and information and develop their findings into mini-reports.

287-289 Computers and Writing

More and more of your students have personal computers, and more and more of your schools are equipped with computer writing labs—which means that more and more of your young writers will want to prepare their writing assignments on computers. What does this mean for you? You must have some firsthand experience composing with a computer and some knowledge of the various word processing programs on the market, so you can answer questions your students may have as they come on-line. Our discussion in this brief chapter provides a good introduction for computers and writing.

Getting Started: If you have access to a computer lab, have your students prepare a brief piece of writing on a computer from start to finish. Then have them list the pluses and minuses of composing with a computer. Make this list the focus of a discussion on computers and writing. Also, read and react to "Computers and Writing" in *Write Source 2000* during this discussion.

Enrichment: Encourage students to practice keyboarding as often as they can. Provide some incentive for practicing—perhaps a certain number of bonus points for 15-30 minutes of practice time.

290-304 Using the Library

This section focuses on the basic information students need in order to use the library: how to use the card catalog, what's included in the reference section (besides the encyclopedias), and how to use the *Readers' Guide*, the thesaurus, and the dictionary. It's up to you and your librarian to point out other types of information and services most libraries have to offer.

Getting Started: Before or after a general discussion of the library, have each student submit a question that they want answered. Something on the order of "How long do mosquitoes live?" not "What is the last word in the third paragraph in chapter fourteen in *Huckleberry Finn*?" "What country has the highest per capita income?" not "What is the most interesting article in a recent issue of *Road & Track* magazine?" Students then pick a question out of a hat to answer, using the resources in the school library. They should present to the class not only an answer (or nonanswer, if that is the case) but also the story of their search.

Enrichment: If at all possible, have your school, community, or university librarian discuss with your students the influence of technology on library services. There are a lot of fascinating things happening in today's libraries because of technology.

Thinking to Learn

Rationale: The opening to "Teaching Thinking in the '90s" (in this guide) discusses in detail why a section in our handbook is devoted to thinking. We make note in that discussion that teachers should teach **for thinking** by creating the right classroom climate, **about thinking** by helping students become more aware of their own thinking, and **of thinking** by teaching thinking skills. Creating the right classroom climate for the teaching of thinking skills is your responsibility. (You'll find plenty of suggestions in "Teaching Thinking in the '90s" to meet these ends.)

In "Thinking to Learn" we've taken on a lot of the responsibility ourselves to help your students become more aware of their own thinking. We identify, among other things, steps students can take to think more carefully, how various levels of thinking apply to the writing they do, and how they can think more creatively and logically.

Chapter Summaries

306-310 Thinking Better

If students are going to improve as thinkers—that is, think more carefully and thoughtfully—they should become more aware of their own thinking process. (You might be familiar with the term *metacognition*. It is a professional buzzword that refers to thinking about thinking.) "Thinking Better" provides an excellent introduction to the fine art of metacogitating. (The section on thinking in this guide suggests a number of ways you can help your students reflect on their thinking.)

Getting Started: Before you have your students read and react to "The Planet of Bad Thinkers," have them create and briefly describe (one paragraph) their own group of bad thinkers—perhaps a classroom of bad thinkers, a team of bad thinkers, a game show for bad thinkers, a ship of fools, and so on. Have them list characteristics of their bad thinkers. Perhaps they never read directions, they let the strongest and best hitter bat first, or they yell out answers before they really know the complete question.

Enrichment: Refer to the last two pages in the thinking section, "Using Your Brain." Talk about the brain: how it works, the whole left brain/right brain issue, the different thinking phases we go through. If at all possible, team up with a science teacher, a local doctor, or a brain specialist and make this a real "whole brain" activity.

Note: Check your school or local library for videotapes of special public television programs on the brain.

311-330 Thinking and Writing

Carnegie Foundation President Ernest Boyer has stated, "Clear writing leads to clear thinking; clear thinking is the basis of clear writing." He, along with any number of individuals connected with education, recognizes the special interrelationship between clear thinking and effective writing. You can't have one without the other. To help your students grow as thinkers and writers, consider implementing writing activities that gradually increase in reasoning complexity and discuss the level(s) of reasoning or thinking required for each activity.

If this is too prescriptive for you, at least be aware of the type of thinking involved in each type of writing activity you assign and make sure your students are aware of this as well. For many writing activities, it's not enough to let students know what they are supposed to do. You should also let them know how they are supposed to carry out the activity by helping them understand the type of thinking involved.

Getting Started: Have students briefly describe the most challenging thinking tasks they have ever performed. Perhaps one student memorized a lengthy list of difficult terms. Another student may have helped design the perfect tree house for his little brother, and still another student may have organized and classified a cardboard box full of family photographs. Use this activity as a lead-in to a discussion of the different levels of thinking. (Refer to "Thinking About Questions and Answers," 330, during your discussion.)

Enrichment: If you have students write in journals, periodically provide them with writing prompts that promote certain levels of thinking—especially those levels of thinking you want to emphasize throughout the school year. For example, a prompt like "A classmate I will never forget" emphasizes basic recall and understanding. A prompt like "What if I never forgot" emphasizes speculating, a more complex level of thinking.

331-342 Thinking Creatively

How can you promote creative thinking and writing in your classroom? First of all, plan classroom activities that promote creative thinking skills like fluency, flexibility, elaboration, and originality. And secondly, encourage your students to think open-endedly and to take risks in your classroom. A creative thinker is not a one-way thinker always looking for right answers. "Thinking Creatively" describes the creative mind in action and works well as an introduction to creative thinking and writing.

Getting Started: To promote open-ended and original thinking, have your students focus on one (or more) of the questions asked in "What if . . . ?" (334) and generate as many answers as they can. A variation: Have pairs of students alternate answers and work from each other's creative thinking.

Enrichment: Have your students complete the minilesson "Can't See the Monkeys from the Bus" (page 150) in this guide. This lesson will really get them thinking and writing creatively.

343-355 Thinking Logically

Who is a good thinker? According to Allan A. Glatthorn and Jonathan Baron in *Developing Minds*, a good thinker is someone who welcomes problematic situations and is tolerant of ambiguity. A good thinker is someone who is reflective and deliberative, someone who believes in the value and the power of logic. And a good thinker is someone who searches and researches until he or she is satisfied that a goal has been reached, or a question has been answered.

This is all pretty heady stuff, especially when you think in terms of your students. But they are all potentially "good thinkers," and, in their own way and to the best of their ability, will become so with the proper guidance and experience. This chapter provides you and your students with a good introduction to the process of logical thinking and also provides your students with an excellent guide for writing clearly and logically.

Getting Started: Have some "good thinkers"—maybe a panel of good thinkers—speak to your class. Perhaps you could have a local attorney describe how he or she prepares and presents a convincing case. A physician could describe how she makes a diagnosis, prepares and carries out an operation, and proposes a plan for recovery. A car mechanic could describe what it means to "troubleshoot" and share some challenging car problems he has dealt with. A coach could describe how he or she plans a strategy for an upcoming opponent, and so on.

Enrichment: Have pairs or small groups of students stage debates, discussions, or old-fashioned arguments that focus on topical and controversial issues.

The rest of the class should evaluate the debaters' performance. Have them pay special attention to the strength of each debater's argument. (Refer them to 344-355 for guidelines.)

Reading TO Learn

Rationale: When students are asked to read to learn, they are obligated to tackle unfamiliar subjects and to address a wide spectrum of supplemental materials.

Therefore, this section has been included to help students meet these reading challenges, to discover strategies to aid their reading comprehension, and to help them remember information.

The four reading-to-learn strategies that are presented in the first chapter, plus the vocabulary-building techniques also included in this section, will help students become independent learners. Once they have received instruction and guided practice, they can use these strategies without your help and study-read more effectively.

"Reading is to the mind what exercise is to the body."
—RICHARD STEELE

Chapter Summaries

361-370 Study-Reading Skills

KWL is a simple yet effective study-reading strategy. It can be used as a prereading activity to create anticipation by asking students to complete the "K" and "W" columns. It becomes an encouraging wrap-up for a unit when students complete the "L" column.

The next two strategies, mapping (364) and word pictures (365), are very popular with middle-school learners. Mapping (sometimes called mind maps or webs) can be used before, during, or after students read. It helps them organize content, formulate concepts, and focus on the key words. It helps students distinguish between the main point and supporting details. Building a map while you and your students brainstorm about reading material helps you assess what your students already know and gives you the advantage of building on their prior knowledge.

Organizing and Verbalizing

Word pictures are graphic organizers that help students reconstruct their textbook reading. Word pictures are effective ways for middle school students to take notes because they help students overcome two common difficulties: deciding what to include and how to organize it. (See topic numbers 413-417 for additional information about note taking.)

Although the **SQ3R** method (366) may look complex, highly motivated readers often rely on SQ3R more than any other study reading method. It shows students that reading to learn is a process and includes one of the most powerful ways to comprehend: verbalizing.

To build interest in SQ3R, we suggest that students make note cards, flash cards, and illustrations as the final step in the process. Sharing note cards works especially well when reviewing.

The guidelines for reading to learn (367-369) provide valuable common sense tips. Teachers in all content areas can direct their students to this page at the beginning of the year to help them develop personal learning plans. At the end of a unit or semester, this page can serve as a guide to help students discover what they are doing well and what they could do better.

Getting Started: To help students experience these personal reading and learning tools, introduce a new strategy or particular word picture each week. Ask them to use these strategies as often as possible throughout the day. Hold deskside conferences to provide students with feedback that will help them refine their work. Comparing their results in small groups is another way to reinforce how effectively these strategies are working for students.

Enrichment: Ask students to create a "How to Learn" booklet, describing and illustrating methods of learning they have found effective. These booklets could be shared with other classrooms or younger students. Students could visit other classrooms and show students firsthand how to use one (or more) of the learning techniques they have found helpful.

371-384 Improving Vocabulary

For students to improve their vocabulary, they must do a number of things: read often, read a lot of different things, come to appreciate and value the richness of words, and become familiar with the parts of words (prefixes, suffixes, and roots).

Getting Started: List one or two words of your choice on the board. Discuss these words, asking students to try to define each one and use it in a sentence. Then have them explore each word in a dictionary and/or thesaurus. Continue the discussion until students have gained a full appreciation of the words. Encourage (or expect) students to investigate vocabulary on their own with the same thoroughness and to record their findings in a vocabulary notebook (372).

Enrichment: On a regular basis, have students present interesting words to the class, words that they have come across in their own reading, listening, and viewing. They may want to organize their presentation in the following ways: *where I came across the word, how it is used,* and *what I found out about it.*

Note: Students may want to refer to 270 in the handbook for more information about sharing the story of a personal research project.

> "Words fascinate me. They always have. For me, browsing in a dictionary is like being turned loose in a bank."
>
> —EDDIE CANTOR

374-384 Prefixes, Suffixes, and Roots

Word parts—prefixes (374-376), suffixes (377), and roots (378-384)—are invaluable bits of information, but your students may not see it this way. Telling them that these little bits of information will help them build an impressive vocabulary may not do much good either. You will have to show them—that is, actually put these word parts to use in activities—before they will appreciate their value. (See pages 121-123 in this guide for ideas.)

385-387 Kinds of Literature and Elements of Literature

The general kinds of literature as well as any of the elements your students may need to know are included in these two lists. Make a master list of literary types and terms you want your students to know; then refer them to the two handbook lists for definitions and examples.

Note: These lists can be helpful when students are reading or studying literature and when they are writing book reviews.

Speaking and Listening to Learn

Rationale: Speaking is language in action, language played out in its most natural state. It is the one aspect of language in which your students are most at ease, most confident, most capable (unless, of course, they're speaking in foreign territory like your classroom).

We applaud you if speaking is an important part of your language arts program. You know how it can motivate your students, enliven your classroom, and enhance learning. You also know that it is just as important, perhaps even more important than the study of writing and reading and grammar.

We encourage the rest of you to give speaking more playing time in your classes, and not just in late-inning relief appearances either. Put it right in your starting rotation. Speaking is much too valuable to play a secondary role.

We also encourage you to incorporate technology into your speaking and listening program. Allow students to record dramatic readings, have them produce video presentations, and give them the opportunity to speak to the student body on the school's P.A. system. As you know, students find all types of technology very attractive.

Your students will find "Speaking and Listening to Learn" especially helpful when they develop formal speeches, prepare oral readings, and conduct interviews. Also included are guidelines for speaking's battery mate—listening.

> *"I believe that every child begins with the drive to explore the world he is born into, that curiosity is indeed 'native.' Speech becomes its principal instrument."*
>
> —JAMES BRITTON

Chapter Summaries

389-398 Preparing a Speech

Mark Twain once said, "It usually takes me more than three weeks to prepare a good impromptu speech." In his classic tongue-in-cheek style, Twain is telling us that for most occasions speaking is much more than standing on a soapbox and ad-libbing. Speaking is thinking and writing and rehearsing and then presenting. That's how we approach preparing a speech in this chapter—as a deliberate process that involves a good deal of planning and preparation. Your students will find the advice, guidelines, and helpful hints easy to follow and effective.

Getting Started: Here is an effective warm-up activity. Have students interview someone in the class whom they don't know very well. Encourage them to be creative in the types of questions they ask: What three things have you never done? What will be your address in 20 years?

Using the guidelines in this chapter, each student should then develop a brief introductory speech to present to the class. Point out that the manner in which they "introduce" their subject is up to them. They may want to develop a campaign speech, make a toast, file charges, etc.

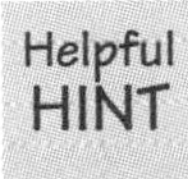

Remind your students that whenever one student is speaking, the rest of the class should be listening. Refer them to the listening skills (402) whenever you feel it is appropriate.

Enrichment: Have your students observe and evaluate experienced speakers in action. (Use videotapes of speakers if in-person observations are impossible.) Review the speaking and listening guidelines in the handbook with your students before the speech presentation.

Note: Make every effort to have speakers visit your classroom. There are any number of individuals in every community willing to contribute their time and effort if you just ask them.

400-401 Reading to Others

When actors and actresses audition for a part, they often are given a script to rehearse and read. They prepare for their audition in much the same way your students should prepare for an oral reading. Make this connection for your students, and they might look at oral reading in a new light . . . with more enthusiasm. Then share with them the guidelines in "Reading to Others" before they get to work on their own scripts.

Getting Started: Make a variety of possible reading selections available to your students. Get your librarian to help you. Consider short plays, poems, song lyrics, dramatic excerpts from short stories and novels, newspaper and magazine articles, letters, diaries, etc. Remind students to select a script that would interest them if they were on the other end—that is, if they were the listener.

Enrichment: Have your students prepare oral readings for a specific audience—the PTA, younger elementary students, the student body of your school, a senior citizen's group, etc.

405-407 Interviewing

We feel that it's important for you to break down the walls of your classroom, so to speak, and help your students see the connection between what they are doing in school and what goes on in the real world. That's why we've included a brief chapter on "Interviewing." It is a very effective way for students to make contact "with the outside."

Getting Started: Students need to see and hear an effective interview in action, so give them one. That is, "stage" an interview for them. Perhaps you could be the subject of the interview, and a fellow teacher could be the interviewer.

Enrichment: Use the minilesson "Mind if I tape this?" on page 149 in this guide to give everyone some firsthand interviewing experience.

Learning to Learn

Rationale: There are four general learning areas covered in this part of the handbook: classroom skills, test taking, group skills, and individual skills. The section on classroom skills focuses on using learning logs and taking notes. The section on group skills provides guidelines for collaborative learning. The information on test taking suggests ways students can effectively prepare for and complete different types of exams. The section on learning skills offers tips for setting goals, managing time, and managing stress. By using this section in the handbook, you can help students develop the skills, interests, and attitudes they will need in their lifelong pursuit of learning.

> *"If we succeed in giving the love of learning, the learning itself is sure to follow."*
>
> —JOHN LUBBOCK

Chapter Summaries

409-417 Classroom Skills

Keeping a learning log is one of the best classroom activities for enhancing learning. It gets students actively involved in the learning process It personalizes learning and helps students make new concepts part of their own thinking.

Getting Started:

Step 1: Explain to students that learning logs are a place for them to think . . . an academic log. They will become mathematicians, historians, scientists, and researchers when they work in their learning logs. They will explore their thoughts to discover more about the data, processes, events, people, and concepts they meet in their texts. They will include opinions, attitudes, insights, and questions.

Step 2: Each day for the first week or two, show students a technique they can use in their academic logs. (Refer students to topic numbers 412-417 in their handbooks.) Choose techniques that students will find most useful in the discipline you are teaching. The following is a sample of general techniques that will work in most classes:

Day 1: KWL (topic 363)
Day 2: Compare and Contrast Word Picture (topic 365)
Day 3: Listing (page 113 in this guide)
Day 4: Mapping (topic 364)
Day 5: Focused Writings (page 112 in this guide)

Step 3: You can also provide an occasional "prompt." ("What if . . ." and "Why" questions serve well as prompts.) Sometimes you may want to use a more specific question, especially if students are learning a system or process they will need again and again. Here are some examples of specific prompts: (1) Describe how you think some insects become butterflies. (2) Brainstorm to compile a list of words concerning ancient Rome and Greece. (3) Pretend you are crossing the Potomac with George Washington. Write an entry in your log as if you were one of the soldiers in the boat. (4) We'll be taking an imaginary trip to Venezuela. List at least five questions you would like to find answers to while you are there. (5) If you could stand on Mars, what do you think you would see?

Step 4: Ask students to write at different times: the beginning of class, the end of class, and various points in between.

Step 5: Use one of the following methods to share thoughts:

- Ask each student to read his or her journal entry in a small group. Group members can make comments, discuss, and ask questions.
- Quickly go around the room, letting each student read her or his entry.
- Publish a list of comments from student entries and give each student a copy.

"On this October morning I asked them to open their new journals to the first page where, as usual, they entered the date and time. Then I directed them: 'Think about and list as many different, unusual ways that we might write in math.' "

—ANNE THOMPSON

The Working Parts

Learning logs (academic journals) are most often spiral-bound notebooks where students are asked to list, free-write, chart, create word pictures, observe, speculate, map, brainstorm, ask questions, role-play, activate prior knowledge, compose a wish list, summarize, paraphrase, predict, connect, create new insights, pose theories, write a letter to a teacher, and so on.

Learning logs should not be graded or corrected. However, every student should be expected to write, and sharing entries is especially productive. Students will be very curious about what other students are thinking. They will gather more data, hear different interpretations, and expand their knowledge when they listen to what classmates write.

Enrichment: Suggest related activities, topics, or prompts to stimulate critical thinking in their learning logs.

- ☐ Have them write a poem using some of the new information covered in class.
- ☐ Have them speculate about the real value or importance of concepts they are studying.
- ☐ Have them present new information to a younger audience, perhaps with accompanying pictures.
- ☐ Have them list different ways they could use their new information.

418-431 Taking Tests

Taking tests is another way to learn (and not just a way to show what has already been learned). This attitude helps both instructors and students use testing wisely. As more and more educators use whole language and performance-based learning, testing is becoming an important avenue for discovering meaning. Such an attitude is the opposite of telling some students they learned the material in exactly the right way (A+) and telling other students they didn't learn anything (F).

There should always be time after testing to help every student relearn everything he/she missed. When students have mastered the content, they can help other students locate and read supplemental materials or do enrichment activities. These choices will offer valuable practice time for interactive and oral skills.

Getting Started: Ask students to write 5-10 objective questions using the information in the handbook as a guide (428-431). These questions can form the basis for a review or be used in an actual test. Students can do the same for essay tests using the key words found at topic numbers 422 and 423.

Enrichment: Ask another teacher to loan you some essay tests he/she has used in the past. Let your students practice their test-taking skills and meet in small groups to discuss which answers or parts of answers best complete the questions.

432-449 Group Skills

Any classroom will function better if you encourage your students to use group skills. As teachers, we have become more and more aware (1) that students can learn from each other, (2) that employers want people who know and practice group skills, and (3) that making our classrooms mentally and emotionally safe places for our students increases their chances of learning. Insisting that students practice groups skills makes these three objectives possible.

Getting Started: Read independently or as a class "Skills for Cooperating" in the handbook (437-441). Next, form small groups and ask students to share entries from their learning logs. While they share and discuss, ask them to practice these skills. Afterward, you may ask them to make a learning log entry about their small-group experiences and how they feel about cooperative skills.

Enrichment: The people skills listed in this section of the handbook, as well as many others, can be identified in literature and history. Ask students to watch for people using group skills well and not so well in their course work. Who encounters greater conflicts because of poor people skills? Who uses people skills to make others feel better and resolve conflicts?

450-457 Individual Skills

On one of the first days of class, let your students know you care about them not only as learners but as people by introducing them to this section of the handbook. By letting your students know you care, you create a safer environment for them and you make it easier for them to relax and pursue learning.

Getting Started with Time Management: Ask your students to create a weekly planner in their learning log and record data for one week. Using this data they can then create a "personal" weekly planner for the remainder of the year.

Getting Started with Stress Management: Ask students to make a journal entry about their level of personal stress. They should consider causes, symptoms, and ways to realistically reduce some of their stress.

Enrichment: Ask students to locate and read more articles and books about time and/or stress management.

> "If there is one conclusion to be drawn which cuts across all the studies, it is this: the more time spent analyzing grammar as grammar, the less time spent writing; the less time spent writing, the less improvement in the written product."
>
> —SARA D'ELOIA

THE Yellow Pages

Rationale: You will note that we've placed "The Yellow Pages" near the end of the handbook. This is to emphasize the fact that writing shouldn't begin with the study of grammar.

You will also note that "The Yellow Pages" are color coded, so it will be easy for your students to flip to this section when they have a question about mechanics, usage, spelling, or grammar. We want your students to run their fingers through this section often.

Study after study has shown that grammar instruction has little or no bearing on a student's ability to communicate effectively. Students learn to write by putting pen to paper—not by memorizing grammatical rules and labeling sentences.

Our intention here is not to downplay the importance of grammar. We know as well as you do that your students must have an appreciation of the standard conventions of our language. However, we do suggest that you put the study of grammar in proper perspective and not make it the focus of your writing program.

Getting Started and Enrichment: See "What About Grammar?" on page 89 in this guide for alternative approaches to grammar instruction. Also, see the minilessons section in this guide for activities related to "The Yellow Pages."

THE Student Almanac

Rationale: We want your students to use *Write Source 2000* in all of their classes as a guide for their writing and learning. But we also want your students to think of the handbook as a general, all-school reference book. That's why we've developed "The Student Almanac." Students will find the many tables, maps, and historical documents helpful in their math, science, geography, and social studies classes.

Getting Started: Have students list all of their classes across the top or along the side of a piece of notebook paper. Then, have them identify parts of "The Student Almanac" that will help them in each of their classes. Also, ask them to identify other parts of the handbook that will help them across the curriculum.

Enrichment: Use "The Student Almanac" as a starting point for "cultural literacy" minilessons. Find one of the many lists detailing what literate Americans need to know. Select people, places, and ideas from such a list in "The Student Almanac" or elsewhere in *Write Source 2000*. Form questions (like those below) that students answer using their handbooks: Where is Puerto Rico? What is a centimeter? What does the Preamble to the Constitution mean to you? When did the Panama Canal open? Proceed from there with a discussion of the questions and the students' answers.

Helpful HINT

Make sure that teachers in all disciplines are aware of all of the valuable information in *Write Source 2000*. And encourage all teachers to make use of the handbook with their students. *Write Source 2000* improves with use.

Writing Programs

The contemporary writing programs described on the following pages offer you an opportunity to use a variety of approaches to meet the individual needs of your students.

An Overview

Contemporary Writing Programs

How were you taught to write?

Did your teachers approach writing as a series of skills that had to be learned sequentially? Did they provide literary models that you were to emulate in your own writing? Or, did they perhaps assign compositions on Mondays with little or no direction and expect flawless, finished copies on Fridays?

Do any of these approaches sound familiar? They should. For years, teachers used these methods to "teach" writing. Consider yourself fortunate if you had teachers who provided you with classrooms conducive to real writing and learning.

How is writing taught today?

If you are up on your contemporary writing research, you know this isn't an appropriate question. Writing isn't really taught. That is, writing isn't a set of facts, forms, or formulas that a teacher imparts, and it certainly isn't worksheet busywork. We now know that it is (or should be) a student-centered activity that is learned through a variety of shared writing experiences.

So where does this put the teacher? Not behind a desk lecturing or correcting yesterday's assignments. It puts her or him right alongside the students; teachers and students write and learn together.

And if writing is not taught, then how is it learned? There are a number of contemporary approaches that promote writing as a student-centered learning activity. All of these approaches have a number of things in common in addition to being student centered.

First of all, writing programs don't require a textbook.

Most textbooks by their very nature are prescriptive. That is, they are designed as much to tie students and teachers to the textbook as they are to help students develop as independent thinkers and writers. In a contemporary writing classroom, the students' own writing serves as the textbook.

Second, the new writing programs are individualized.

In most contemporary writing classrooms, students work and learn individually and in small groups. Instruction is based on need and given when one or more students need help with a basic skill or rhetorical concept. The form of the instruction is usually a 10- to 15-minute minilesson. (See page 133 in this guide for information on minilessons.) Full-class activities are kept to a minimum.

They are lively and active.

Modern writing programs promote active learning. On any given day, students might spend their time in a group-critiquing session or writing or reading on their own or helping classmates sort out problems with their work. There's no hiding in the last row of the classroom as the teacher lectures.

They are well planned.

Just because contemporary writing programs are student centered doesn't mean that students can simply do as they please. Even the most motivated students will take advantage of too much freedom. Deadlines, support materials, methods of instruction, methods for measuring writing progress, and sensible classroom management procedures all have to be established for a program to be successful. Programs must also be flexible enough to meet the needs and interests of the students (obviously within reason) as the course work progresses.

They are integrated.

Finally, contemporary writing programs draw from all of the significant research. A particular program won't, for example, be based solely on the writing process approach or on whole language learning. Instead, it will most likely be a blend or combination of approaches. What follows is a brief description of four of the most significant approaches to writing.

Five Approaches to Writing

> *"Writing to me is a voyage, an odyssey, a discovery, because I'm never certain of precisely what I will find."*
>
> —GABRIEL FIELDING

1 The "Process" Approach

While using the process approach, students learn that writing—real writing—is a process of discovery and exploration rather than an end product or a series of basic skills. As students develop their writing, they make use of all steps in the writing process—prewriting, writing the first draft, revising, proofreading, and publishing. And the writing they develop, for the most part, stems from their own thinking and experiences.

Students use prewriting activities to discover writing ideas they know and care about. They are encouraged to talk about their ideas and create a community of writers within the classroom. They write first drafts freely and quickly, and they revise carefully. After editing and proofreading, students share or publish their work.

Write Source 2000 includes a complete discussion of the writing process. (See 011.) You will note that we refer to prewriting activities as *selecting* and *collecting*, writing and revising as *connecting*, editing and proofreading as *correcting*. Also, note that the guidelines for the specific types of writing are organized according to the steps in the writing process. (See pages 62-63 in this guide for more on the writing process.)

2 The Whole Language (Thematic) Approach

When using the whole language approach, the teacher (ideally with student input) chooses a theme that serves as the focal point for an intense and thorough whole language experience—that is, an experience that immerses students in a variety of integrated reading, writing, listening, and speaking activities.

The teacher provides pieces of literature and other prewriting activities as starting points for the thematic study. Writing projects evolve from these activities. The writing process approach and usually some form of the writing workshop approach are incorporated into whole language programs.

The *Write Source 2000 Language Series* includes a number of whole language writing units for grades 6, 7, and 8. (See pages 64-65 in this guide for more on whole language learning.)

3 The Personal Experience Approach

The focus of this approach is simple: Students enjoy writing and find it meaningful if it stems from their personal experiences and observations. Students usually keep a journal in a personal experience (experiential) program so they always have a number of potential writing ideas to draw from. As with most contemporary approaches, the writing process and some form of a writing workshop are incorporated into the program.

Free writing (rapid writing, spontaneous writing) plays an integral part in this approach to writing as well. Both journal writing and free writing help students write honestly and sincerely about their personal experiences in assigned writing. And it helps students eventually produce writing that readers will find interesting and entertaining.

Review the table of contents in *Write Source 2000*, and you will note that we generally address personal forms of writing before we address more detached, content-oriented forms of writing. It follows that the more students write from personal experience, the better able they are to address increasingly more complex experiences in more sophisticated forms of writing. This writing eventually becomes more and more public, the kind of writing students are often forced to produce long before they're ready.

See *Student-Centered Language Arts K-12* by James Moffett and Betty Jane Wagner (Heinemann-Boynton/ Cook, 1992) for more on this approach.

> "Some students don't accept the invitation [to write] as readily. They need to find out who they are as learners. They need to find out who I am as a learner, and how I will respond and react to what they know. They need to know me as a person. They need to trust me. We need to know and trust each other. It takes time."
>
> —LINDA RIEF

4 The Writing Workshop Approach

In a writing workshop, students write or work on writing-related issues every day (reading, researching, critiquing, participating in collaborative writing, etc.). They are expected to keep all of their work in writing folders, and they are expected to produce a predetermined number of finished pieces by the end of the term. They are encouraged to take risks, to experiment with new forms and techniques. Support during each writing project comes from both peer and teacher conferences. Students utilize the steps in the writing process to develop their writing and share their work with the group.

The teacher acts as a guide and facilitator. She or he creates a classroom environment that is conducive to the workshop approach. Desks and chairs are arranged to make student interaction easy. The classroom is stocked with an ample supply of relevant reading and writing materials. Instruction and advice are given as they are needed on an individual basis, in small groups, or to the entire class. Instruction generally takes the form of a minilesson. The teacher also serves as the final editor before a piece is published.

See pages 67-68 in this guide for more information about writing workshops. Also refer to *In the Middle* by Nancie Atwell (Heinemann-Boynton/Cook, 1987) for a discussion of a middle-school workshop program in action.

5 The Cross-Curricular Approach

When a writing-across-the-curriculum program is implemented, students begin to experience writing as an important part of the learning process. The types of writing students do will vary from subject to subject and from situation to situation. In one class, students may be freely recording their observations about a new concept. In another class, students may be summarizing a magazine article. And in still another class, students may be writing news stories.

Planning is the key to a successful across-the-curriculum writing program. Content-area teachers should have an understanding of the basic reasons to write: to share information, to show learning, to better understand new ideas, and to explore personal thoughts and feelings. And they should give students opportunities to write for all of these reason. Teachers must also know how to plan writing assignments that challenge and stimulate students. It's not enough to have them write an occasional paragraph. In order to grow as writers, students must be provided with meaningful assignments that encourage risk taking and experimentation.

Instructional Resources

The *Write Source 2000* handbook serves as an excellent student resource for cross-curricular writing. It provides guidelines and models for many forms of writing. It discusses the writing process, writing to learn, and journal writing. It offers a complete proofreader's guide to help students take writing to finished form. The handbook makes it possible for all teachers to become writing teachers.

This guide also contains a great deal of information related to writing across the curriculum starting on page 69. Included in this discussion are prompts for cross-curricular journal writing, guidelines for designing effective writing assignments, and lists of ideas for content-area writing projects. Also see "Writing to Learn" (pages 110-113) in this guide for many easy-to-implement writing activities that help students make new information part of their own thinking.

The "Process" Approach

1. What is writing?

- Writing is thinking on paper.
- Writing is "chasing thinking and turning it into thought."
- Writing is "the exposed edge of thought."

2. What is the "writing process"?

- The "writing process" is the best way we know of to turn thinking into writing.
- The process is usually broken down into four or five manageable steps, allowing students to concentrate on one step at a time.
- The steps in the process are generally broken down into prewriting, writing, revising, proofreading, and publishing.

3. Why do students write?

(Traditional Objectives)

- To demonstrate the retention of information.
- To improve language skills, especially surface skills (punctuation, handwriting, spelling, . . .).
- To please the teacher.

(Using the Writing Process)

- To explore and to understand their world.
- To learn, to discover, to clarify thinking.
- To pass along information.

4. How is writing encouraged?

(Teacher-Centered Approach)

- Assign a topic, length, time limit.
- Assign an outline and/or "thesis statement."
- Assign an introduction; check for compliance.
- Expect students to produce a "correct" paper.
- Mark, grade, comment.
- Return papers, marked for all errors.
- Request that some students rewrite their assignments until they get them right.

(Student-Centered Approach)

- Students use prewriting activities to discover a topic they know and care about. (See 033-038 in *Write Source 2000* for examples.)
- Students are encouraged to "talk" about their topics to help them develop a sense of purpose for writing.
- Students write for real audiences—usually their peers—rather than for their teachers.
- When students write a first draft, they focus on getting ideas down on paper.
- They think as they go, crossing out, switching directions, using abbreviations, writing rapidly.
- Students revise their writing by going back over what they have written—adding, cutting, replacing, and moving information.
- They read aloud what they have written and discuss it with their peers and/or teacher.
- At this stage, the focus is on ideas, order, clarity, word choice, ways to make the piece more exciting. (See 021 in *Write Source 2000* for more.)
- Students proofread their work only after they have their ideas straight.
- Students work on mechanical problems in small groups, in individual conferences, with the whole class, or by using a handbook of mechanics and usage.
- Students keep their papers until they are ready to share them; then they put their writing in finished form.
- Students publish their work—which might simply mean that their writing is displayed for peers to read.
- The teacher, with student input, grades the finished product.

5. What are the results of using the writing process?

- Students find writing more meaningful because it becomes a reflection of their own thinking.
- Students develop a feel for real writing.
- Students develop independent thinking skills and take pride in their work.
- Students develop a better attitude toward writing, which results in better writing from students of all abilities.
- Using the writing process means less work for teachers.

6. What do current guides to curriculum planning say about writing and the writing process?

(We happen to be located in Wisconsin. Our DPI produces an excellent guide to curriculum planning from which the following information was taken.)

The Language Arts Task Force recommends the following about writing:

- Curriculum and instruction in writing reflect the knowledge that we learn language holistically, through whole problems in creating meaning, rather than through practice in isolated skills.
- Texts reinforce and support the teaching that has already gone on within the writing process.
- Writing should be a schoolwide activity, integrated into content-area learning at all levels.
- Students at all levels do original writing every week, gaining consistent experience in working through the entire writing process.
- Teachers view writing as a developmental process rather than an accumulation of skills.
- Curriculum and instruction recognize the contribution of current research and effective classroom practice.
- Each district should develop a consistent K-12 philosophy for the teaching of writing.

The Task Force also recognizes the following:

- "Grammar" ought to be taught in the context of actual oral and written communication.
- Sentence diagramming, labeling parts of speech, and having students memorize lists of rules are traditional practices that should be avoided.
- Sentence combining, sentence expansion, and sentence transformation are worthwhile classroom practices.
- Students must be taught how to revise, then given regular opportunities to practice.

7. Why is it important for all teachers to know about the writing process?

- When implemented properly, it can change the effectiveness of the entire school system—in all areas.
- A districtwide implementation of the writing process would provide continuity within the K-12 writing program.
- Using the writing process in all its forms significantly enhances learning in all subjects.
- The writing process works well with all forms of learning, especially thinking and cooperative learning.

The Whole Language Approach

Whole language isn't just for language arts teachers. Teachers of music, social studies, art, math, or any other subject can also be whole language teachers. By integrating reading, writing, speaking, and listening activities into specific content areas, teachers can provide students with whole language experiences, ones that will actively involve them in learning.

Here's how teachers can apply whole language the whole day:

Incorporate reading . . .

- Provide plenty of reading material relevant to your subject area. (Magazines, journals, and biographies are great resources.)
- Within certain limits, allow students to choose their own reading material.
- Give time for SSR (sustained silent reading).
- Provide students time to react to and share their reading.
- Encourage the reading of a wide variety of research materials that are authentic and meaningful; also encourage personal interviews, site visits, and discussions with friends and relatives (from which subsequent recommendations and motivation for reading may come). (See 360-387 in *Write Source 2000* for more information.)

Incorporate listening . . .

- Make listening an important part of the daily activities.
- Practice listening techniques and help students develop skills for effective listening.
- Build listening skills within the context of daily activities; avoid using too many isolated drills and exercises.
- Encourage students to interview people they (the students) are interested in.
- Arrange for speakers who are willing to tell their stories and share their experiences.
- Help students identify each speaker's purpose and their own purpose for listening. (See 402 in the handbook for more information and the *Write Source 2000 Language Program* for student activities.)

Incorporate writing . . .

- Allow students the freedom to choose what they want to write.
- Provide students with examples of interesting writing.
- Promote writing as a process (rather than a set of skills or an end product).
- Let students write for different audiences: classmates, contest judges, newspaper and magazine editors, friends and relatives.
- Use writing-to-learn activities: journal writing, learning logs, stop 'n' write, exit slips, admit slips, etc. Writing-to-learn activities are ungraded and free from traditional teacher evaluation. (See 409-412 in the handbook for more information.)

Incorporate speaking . . .

- Provide students with a wide range of speaking opportunities relevant to their interests and experiences.
- Stimulate discussion by asking questions and providing feedback.
- Give students at all levels frequent opportunities to create classroom dramas.
- Make use of video and audio equipment, filmstrips, overhead projectors, computers, and other technological equipment. (See 388-407 in the handbook for more information on incorporating speaking into classroom activities.)

Here's how whole language teachers approach learning in their classrooms:

- You'll find teachers and students working together as active participants in the learning process.
- Writing, reading, speaking, and listening are everyday tools for learning.
- Teachers see reading, writing, speaking, and listening as complementary strands of language learning, and incorporate them throughout the day.
- The students' personal classroom experiences are open-ended, shaped by their input.
- Teachers provide opportunities for students to connect with real-life events.
- There is shared decision making. Everyone participates in the decision-making process, including decisions about materials, activities, and evaluation.

> *"The secret of education is respecting the pupil."*
> —RALPH WALDO EMERSON

- Students have opportunities for cooperative learning and peer conferencing (sharing and tutoring).
- There is respect for the ideas and interests of others. It is understood that each learner has something valuable and important to contribute.
- Instruction is student directed; students influence what is talked about and being taught.
- Every child works at his or her ability level and therefore experiences success.
- Activities are considered "invitations" rather than assignments. Students are invited to read, write, and explore topics that are of interest to them.
- Reading, writing, speaking, and listening are integrated to create theme studies across the content areas.
- Errors are considered a source of information rather than a sign of failure. Risk taking produces errors, and students learn by those errors.
- Evaluation is ongoing. Evaluations are made primarily on a personal basis, and each student is seen as unique. Self-evaluation is an important part of the whole language process.
- Teachers observe students and continually evaluate and improve their programs based on those observations.
- For more characteristics of a whole language classroom refer to the following titles:

  What's Whole in Whole Language
  —Ken Goodman

  Whole Language: Theory in Use
  —Judith Newman

  The Whole Language Evaluation Book
  —Edited by Ken and Yetta Goodman and Wendy Hood

> *"A school should not be a preparation for life. A school should be life."*
> —ELBERT HUBBARD

In a whole language classroom students are encouraged to make learning connections "outside" of school.

The Personal Experience Approach

"I can tap into [my students'] human instincts to write if I help them realize that their lives and memories are worth telling stories about, and if I help them zoom in on topics of fundamental importance to them."

—WRITING TEACHER JUNE GOULD

We know from firsthand experience that the personal stories young learners love to share can serve as the basis of an effective and lively writing program. Here's how we did it:

Getting Started

At the beginning of the school year, we introduced in-class journal writing to the students. (We encouraged students to write outside of class in journals as well, but the journals in school were part of our writing program.) We knew that the most effective way to get students into writing was simply to let them write often and freely about their own lives, without having to worry about grades or turning their writing in. This helped them develop a feel for writing, real writing, writing that originates from their own thoughts and feelings.

That's where the journals come in. No other activity that we know of gets students into writing more effectively than personal journal writing. (And no other type of writing is so easy to implement.) All your students need are spiral notebooks, pens, time to write, and encouragement to explore whatever is on their minds. (See 130 in the handbook for more information.)

We provided our students with four or five personal writing prompts each time they wrote. They could use one of these prompts as a starting point for their writing if they wished. The choice was theirs.

Writing Prompts

Here's a typical list of writing prompts: Write about . . .

- a memorable kitchen-related experience,
- coping with younger brothers or sisters,
- being home alone, late at night, or
- what you did over the past weekend.

We would ask our students to write every other day for the first 10 minutes of the class period. Students knew that every Monday, Wednesday, and Friday were writing days..

Keeping It Going

After everyone was seated and roll was taken, the journals were passed out, the prompts were given, and everyone wrote. We expected students to write for the complete 10 minutes nonstop. And we made sure that they did. They knew that they would be given a quarter journal grade for the number of words they produced. This made a contest out of the writing sessions. Each time they wrote, they wanted to see if they could increase their production from past journal entries.

Wrapping It Up

On days that we weren't writing, we shared journal entries. First, students would exchange journals with a classmate. They would count the number of words in the entry, read it carefully, and then make comments on things they liked or questioned. After they shared their comments among themselves, we would talk about the entries as a class.

The writers themselves would be reluctant to share their entries with the entire class. But the readers had no problem volunteering someone else's entry ("You've got to hear Nick's story") and reading it out loud. The students loved these readings and the discussions that followed.

Personal Experience Papers

Periodically, we would interrupt the normal course of journal writing and sharing and make formal writing assignments. That is, we would ask students to review their entries and select one (or part of one) to develop into a more polished, complete personal experience paper. Usually, those entries that readers enjoyed and wanted to know more about would be the ones the young writers would choose to develop.

We wanted to make sure that their writing went through at least one or two thorough revisions, so we gave our writers plenty of class time to work on their papers. They also were required to turn in all of their preliminary work with their final drafts. (See "Writing About Experiences," 144, in the handbook for guidelines for this type of writing.)

> *"In a very real sense, the writer writes in order to teach himself, to understand himself, to satisfy himself."*
>
> —ALFRED KAZIN

The experience papers were shared with the entire class at the end of the project. This was a fun and informal activity, but one that students came to appreciate as an important part of the entire composing process. It was their day. They were on stage. They were sharing the end product of all of their work—a special moment in their own lives.

The Writing Workshop Approach

See a writing workshop in action by studying the sample schedule on the following page. Here you will find how one teacher organized his writing workshop. This schedule reserves time for minilessons, status checks, individual or group work, and sharing sessions.

Since this schedule is designed for one of the first weeks of a workshop, all students are asked to participate in the minilessons. In time, you can meet the needs of your students by inviting only those attempting certain goals to do minilessons. All other students will be actively engaged with a piece of writing or another option you have offered.

Instructor Checklist— A Management Tool

One management technique that teachers of workshops advocate is the use of a checklist similar to the one shown on the right. The teacher designs the checklist after he or she has set up a weekly schedule. Such a checklist serves as a quick reference for you as the week unfolds, and as a history as the year proceeds.

Sample Checklist

- ☐ Cover minilessons.
  - ☐ 011, 012, 013 (Introduction to writing process and choosing a subject)
  - ☐ 035-036 (Activities to help discover and select a subject)
  - ☐ 130-132 (Journal keeping)
  - ☐ 020 (Writing the first draft)
- ☐ Teach two reading-to-learn strategies.
  - ☐ Tell/retell
  - ☐ Smart
- ☐ All students receive writing folders.
- ☐ Students experiment with free writing and clustering.
- ☐ Students make three journal entries.
- ☐ Students work on a first draft.
- ☐ Students write exit slips.

Writing Workshop: Weekly Schedule

This schedule can vary depending on the teacher's needs. A teacher might, for example, conduct writing workshops for three days a week and reading workshops for the other two days. (See page 99 in this guide for a schedule for the first week in a reading workshop.)

MONDAY	TUESDAY	WEDNESDAY	THURSDAY	FRIDAY
Writing Minilesson 10 MIN.	**Writing Minilesson** 10 MIN.	**Writing Minilesson** 10 MIN.	**Writing Minilesson** 10 MIN.	**Quiz Review of Minilessons** 10 MIN.
Status Check 2 MIN. (Find out what students will work on for the day.)	**Status Check** 2 MIN. (Find out what students will work on for the day.)	**Status Check** 2 MIN. (Find out what students will work on for the day.)	**Status Check** 2 MIN. (Find out what students will work on for the day.)	**Status Check** 2 MIN. (Find out what students will work on for the day.)
Individual Work Writing, Revising, Editing, Conferencing, or Publishing 30 MIN.	**Individual Work** Writing, Revising, Editing, Conferencing, or Publishing 30 MIN.	**Individual Work** Writing, Revising, Editing, Conferencing, or Publishing 30 MIN.	**Individual Work** Writing, Revising, Editing, Conferencing, or Publishing 30 MIN.	**Individual Work** Writing, Revising, Editing, Conferencing, or Publishing 30 MIN.
Whole Class Sharing Session 5 MIN.	**Whole Class Sharing Session** 5 MIN.	**Whole Class Sharing Session** 5 MIN.	**Whole Class Sharing Session** 5 MIN.	**Whole Class Sharing Session** 5 MIN.

The Cross-Curricular Approach

Teaching with Writing . . .

Journal writing, dialogues, stories, and **letters**—these popular forms of writing have traditionally been associated with the language arts curriculum. But not any longer. There are more and more teachers across the curriculum who have their students explore their thoughts and feelings in journals, confront challenging ideas in dialogues, and develop historical and scientific stories. And why so?

These teachers realize that writing plays a central role in the learning process. Writing by its very nature gets students actively and thoughtfully involved in their work whether they are studying algebraic equations, photosynthesis, or local government. It helps them understand and remember important concepts. It makes them more appreciative of course content and curious to learn more. And it gives students control over their own learning.

The Ultimate Learning Tool

Writing is such an important learning tool that all content-area teachers must make room for it in their curriculum. The critical question no longer addresses why students should be writing across the curriculum, but rather how much writing they should be doing and in what forms. That's why we've developed this section. We want to help all teachers make writing an integral part of instruction.

A Few Words About Literacy

Before we go on, another reason for writing across the curriculum should be mentioned. All teachers must do as much as possible to promote **literacy** in their classrooms. We're not referring here to basic writing and reading competency. That no longer is enough. We're looking at literacy in bigger and broader terms.

Students must be equipped to use the language at a proficient level if they are going to become or remain active and interested learners. Without this proficiency, it is next to impossible for students to succeed at any level in any content area (except, perhaps, in the very early years of schooling). How can students display any level of mastery in social studies, for instance, if they can't write, read, or talk about it? Certainly memorizing or recalling a few facts or dates is not enough.

Some experts would say that writing and reading (as well as the other language arts) should be a primary focus of instruction across the curriculum. So many of the abilities we want to instill in students stem from language proficiency: to be responsive and creative learners, to be clear and critical thinkers, to be effective and accurate communicators, and to be resourceful and purposeful readers.

What We Have in Mind

The level of literacy we have in mind can't be achieved unless all teachers in all content areas do their part. Language proficiency demands everyone's attention. We can think of no better way for all teachers at the middle-school level (or otherwise) to pool their efforts and talents than to promote writing and reading. It is a no-lose situation. The more proficient students become as writers and readers, the more able and eager they are to learn.

> *"In the best of all possible worlds, language study should be part and parcel of the entire school curriculum. The whole school day should be a learning workshop."*
>
> —NANCIE ATWELL

Implementing Writing Across the Curriculum

Teachers who are ready to make writing an important part of their curriculum should do four things:

1. Teachers should gain a basic understanding of the writing process and writing instruction. (That can be achieved by reading the first chapter in the *Write Source 2000* handbook as well as the sections on writing in this guide.)
2. They should decide how best to incorporate writing into their curriculum. There are many different reasons to write and many different types of writing to choose from. (More on that later.)
3. They should make changes in their curriculum to accommodate for writing. (Now before anyone cries foul, please know that we're not talking about wholesale changes. We're simply asking teachers to cut back a *little* on course content.)
4. They should serve as role models and write (and read) themselves. This might be the most important thing teachers can do. (Students appreciate teachers who care enough about writing to put pen to paper themselves.)

Reasons to Write

There are many reasons for asking students to write; the four reasons that follow deserve playing time in any writing-across-the-curriculum program:

- **Writing to share learning** has to be another important element in a schoolwide writing program. Students approach writing with more interest, care, and concern if they know that they have an interested audience with whom to share their work. (Generally speaking, in language arts classes writing is approached as a *process* of shaping and reshaping an initial idea into a finished paper ready to share with an audience.)

- **Writing to show learning** is the traditional reason content-area teachers have had their students write. When students compose summary paragraphs, compile reports, or answer essay-test questions, they are writing to show learning. This manner of composing is only one of four reasons to write and, in many ways, not the most important one. (See "Writing Assignments in the Content Areas" later in this discussion for more on these last two reasons to write.)

- **Writing to better understand new concepts and ideas** is one of the most beneficial reasons to have students write (and very easy for teachers to implement). This unrehearsed and ungraded mode of writing helps students make new information part of their own thinking. ***In this way, writing serves as the ultimate learning tool.*** (Refer to "Writing to Learn . . . ," pages 110-113 in this guide, for more information and examples.)

- **Writing to explore personal thoughts and feelings** works as well in social studies or science as it does in language arts. Students who engage in exploratory writing (usually done in a journal or a learning log) become much more in tune with their course work and much more comfortable with the act of composing.

> *"The productive use of language, and especially writing, is a valuable tool for learning for all students in all subjects at all ages."*
>
> —JOHN S. MAYHER, NANCY LESTER, AND GORDON M. PRADL

Writing Prompts for Journals

Teachers who work with journals often provide students with one or two prompts each time they are expected to write. Students are encouraged to use one of the prompts as a starting point for their writing if they wish, or they can write about a topic of their own choosing. (Sample prompts are included on the next page.)

Sample Writing Prompts for Journals

History

- Pretend a new continent was discovered and you are going to settle there. What are five things you'll need to do?
- Why could the Middle Ages also be called the "dark ages"?
- Do you think Charlemagne should have been called "Charles the Great"? Why or why not?

Mathematics

- Explain prime numbers to a friend.
- Why do you think our number system is base 10?
- Write a letter to me that takes me step-by-step through your solution to ____________.
- Write a word problem that will give your classmates practice with the concept of ____________.

Science

- What does "endangered" mean to you?
- If you could stand on the ocean floor, what do you think you'd see?
- How are trees good community members?
- Pretend you're a meteorologist. Explain to a class of third graders what a barometer does.

Social Studies

- Write about the cave paintings depicted in your social studies book. You are the artist. What will you say about your creation?
- List 10 questions you'd like answered in our study of ____________.
- If you could change one thing in our community, what would it be?
- "Not all Americans celebrate Thanksgiving." What does this mean to you?

Geography

- What is geography?
- What causes a desert to form?
- What would you like to know about maps and making them?
- Why do you think the earth is hottest at the equator?

Reading and Literature

- Who is your favorite author so far this year? What do you like about this author's writing?
- Tell me about your favorite character in the book you are reading. What kind of person is the character, and why is he/she your favorite?
- How do you think a poem is different from prose?
- Write a letter to me [the teacher] about the book you are reading now.

Writing Assignments in the Content Areas

Content-area teachers often rely on very basic forms of writing for assignments—primarily paragraphs and reports. There's nothing wrong with this standard fare, but there are so many other ways for students to share (or show) what they have learned. They can write historical or science fiction stories, news stories, feature articles, and so on.

Teachers don't have to be accomplished fiction writers, journalists, or technical writers to have students experiment with these different forms of writing. The role of the content-area teachers should be to help students develop their ideas. They (the teachers) are the experts in their respective areas of instruction, and they can put this expertise to good use by guiding students as they select, investigate, and initially work with writing ideas. What's needed to help students shape and refine their writing is a handbook like *Write Source 2000*.

> *"I hear and I forget; I see and I remember; I write and I understand."*
>
> —CHINESE PROVERB

Our Recommendations

Why do we recommend that teachers vary the type of writing they assign? If all we ever ate for lunch were ham and cheese sandwiches, soon we would lose our taste for them. The same holds true for writing. You can't expect students to have much of an appetite for writing if their diet never varies.

There is another reason for this recommendation. Assigning paragraphs and reports generally promotes what James Britton calls "classificatory writing—or writing which reflects information in the form teachers and textbooks present it." Put in another way, the paragraphs and reports students write often reflect what they have been told or what they have read with little personal thought invested in the process.

Opportunities for students to write in more creative and critical ways are needed to complement (or supplement) such assignments. Generally speaking, writing poems, stories, and letters are much more thoughtful enterprises than writing basic paragraphs and reports. These alternative forms demand more commitment on the part of students and get them more intellectually and emotionally involved in their writing. They force students to understand and apply information rather than simply restate it.

Writing for Real Audiences

As stated earlier, students also need every opportunity to write for real audiences, people other than their teachers. Writing letters (to send), editorials (to submit), stories (to read aloud), and plays (to perform) provides such opportunities. When students know that there is a real audience out there, they are more apt to put forth their best efforts. Their writing is a reflection of their very own thinking. It only makes sense that they would want it to reflect as positive an image as possible.

Initiating Writing and Learning

Content-area teachers interested in designing writing assignments that promote writing to learn should carefully read the next two pages. A model assignment, guidelines for getting started, and a reproducible planning sheet are included there. In addition, teachers will find a list of more than 50 ideas for writing across the curriculum, starting on page 76 in this section. These writing ideas cover all the basic content areas, from science and social studies to language arts and mathematics.

And certainly not to be forgotten are all of the ready-made activities promoting writing and learning in the *Write Source 2000 Language Program*. There are enough of these activities to be shared among all the content areas. (See pages 153-163 in this guide for a discussion of the program.

Designing Writing Assignments

Writing Assignment I:

In a paragraph, identify three ways in which consumers can produce less waste.

Discussion: It's a sure bet that students' responses to such an assignment will be very predictable . . . and, unfortunately, very dull. ("There are three main ways to cut down on consumer waste . . .") The assignment follows the age-old formula: question and answer, tell and retell, stimulus and response, fill in the blank. It is limited in scope and intent. It requires little genuine thinking on the part of students, and, therefore, they gain very little from the experience. A meaningful and memorable learning experience it is not. Compare this assignment with the one that follows.

Writing Assignment II:

Convince a friend, parent, or neighbor—real or imagined—that he or she should produce less waste.

Subject: The problem of consumer waste

Audience: The subject of your writing and your reading audience (your writing group or classmates)

Purpose: To convince someone to change his or her behavior

Form: Friendly letter, editorial letter, modern fable . . .

Speaker: You, as a young person concerned about the environment

Guidelines for Evaluation:

- Is the main point of the writing clear?
- Does the writing sound convincing? (Are main points supported by specific details?)
- Does the writing form a meaningful whole, moving smoothly and clearly from one point to the next?
- Will readers appreciate the treatment of this assignment?

Discussion: So many more possibilities are presented to students in the second example. They can't follow a formula or simply repeat what they have already been told or what they have already read. Instead, they have to apply their knowledge about the subject matter in a specific context that they help design. They have to decide whom they are going to address, what they are going to say, and how they are going to say it. It is the type of assignment that can lead to real learning, and it is the type of assignment that should be featured across the curriculum. Study it carefully.

Getting Started

In *Learning to Write/Writing to Learn* (Heinemann-Boynton/Cook, 1983), authors John Mayher, Nancy Lester, and Gordon Pradl provide a basic three-step process to help content-area teachers incorporate well-conceived writing assignments into their curriculum.

Step 1. First, teachers should define or identify learning objectives in their disciplines that could be facilitated by writing. The authors stress that these must be genuine objectives (to help students relate the problem of consumer waste to their immediate world, for instance) rather than activities.

Step 2. They should then design a writing assignment (or task) that would help students achieve a specified objective. (It's important that both the purpose and audience are defined.)

Step 3. Lastly, teachers should establish guidelines or criteria to evaluate the outcome of the students' work. (Evaluation should focus on writing as a process of learning and making meaning.)

Note: A planning sheet is provided on the next page to help teachers design well-conceived writing assignments.

Designing Your Own Assignments

SUBJECT:

AUDIENCE:

PURPOSE:

FORM:

SPEAKER:

* * * * * * * * * * * * * * * * * * *

PREWRITING ACTIVITIES: (Prewriting activities are important if the writing assignment does not stem from information or concepts already covered in the class.)

1.

2.

GUIDELINES FOR EVALUATION: (Emphasize clarity, inventiveness, and depth of thought more than correctness.)

1.

2.

3.

Helping Students . . .

With Writing in General

How can content-area teachers create the proper climate for writing in their classrooms? In *Investigate Nonfiction* (Heinemann, 1989), Donald Graves gives the following advice:

- Allow students to work on their writing in class. Students need sustained periods of time to immerse themselves in their work. (That is why many teachers conduct writing workshops in their classrooms.)
- Reserve class time for sharing sessions. When students have opportunities to talk about their writing in progress, they generally put more effort into their work. (It also helps if they get to write about subjects that genuinely interest them.)
- Encourage (or require) students to keep track of their writing progress, perhaps in journals or log entries. (This helps them maintain interest in their writing.)
- Share writing models so students can see how professionals write about math, science, history, and so on. (Spend some time discussing these models to ensure that students fully appreciate the writing.)

With Report Writing

Teachers can't expect students to come into their classrooms completely knowledgeable about report-writing. They will need a great deal of guidance and practice with the process. Note the following suggestions made by Graves:

- Have students decide what they already know about a subject for a report and what they need to find out it. (This gives students a starting point for their research.)
- Encourage students to use clusters (semantic webs, maps) to sort out their thoughts and feelings about their subject and to help plan and organize their writing.
- Encourage students to work with a subject through at least two sequences of data gathering, discussing, and exploratory writing before they establish a definite form and focus for their report. (Students need to think of report writing as a process of discovery.)
- Initiate more than one report assignment throughout the school year. Some reports can be shorter than others, and not all of them have to be taken to finished form. (Proficiency comes through practice.)

Note: When classroom reports are assigned, make sure students turn to the handbook for guidelines and a model. (Refer to "Report, The Classroom" in the index for this information.)

With Essay Writing

Middle-level students can develop thoughtful essays if teachers provide the necessary foundation for this challenging form of writing. Graves suggests that teachers prepare students in the following ways:

- Look for opportunities to have students tell stories or recount processes. (The ability to recount is strongly connected with the ability to plan and write nonfiction prose.)
- Provide many information-gathering experiences for students. (Interviewing and other firsthand data-gathering experiences like direct observation should be given priority.)
- Ask students to interpret the data they have gathered. (The foundation of effective nonfiction writing is collecting and interpreting data.)
- Consider classroom disagreements and controversies as valuable "teachable moments." (Argumentation is based on differing points of view.)
- Encourage students to write letters filled with facts, feelings, and opinions. (Letter writing is first cousin to essay writing.)

Ideas for Cross-Curricular Writing

What follows are ideas for writing assignments arranged according to content areas. (Each idea is also identified according to grade level.) Included under the heading "A Mixed Bag" are ideas for writing related to the arts, technical education, and so on.

Note: With a few adjustments, many of the ideas listed here will work in more than one content area and in more than one grade level. How they are implemented will ultimately be decided by individual teachers, teaching teams, and the needs and nature of the students.

■ SCIENCE

Weather in Writing

Develop a story, a description, or an explanation about any subject, incorporating aspects of weather in your writing. (6)

In the Wake of the News

Serve as the class science reporter and prepare a summary of one important science-related article in either a daily newspaper or a weekly newsmagazine. (6)

Extra! Extra!

Collect newspaper or magazine articles related to a scientific topic. Use these articles as a starting point for a short report. (6)

But you also have to remember . . .

Study both (or all) sides of a controversial, science-related issue using the Venn diagram as a guide. Compile the results in a paragraph, a letter, or an essay. (Refer to "Venn diagram" in the handbook index for an explanation.) (6)

Dear Benjamin

Write an imaginary letter to an important figure in science, discussing issues pertaining to the individual's accomplishments. (7)

Great Moments in Science Research

Research great moments in science in reference books, magazines, articles, newspapers, and other resources. Use these facts as a starting point for a fictionalized account of the moment. This could take the form of a children's story, a one-act play, a radio drama, and so on. (7)

Mr. or Ms. Wizard

Select a scientific concept (gravity, density, laser light) for a class presentation or speech. Research the subject, write a script, prepare props, and so on. (7)

Travel Brochures

Develop a travel brochure, complete with copy, illustrations, and graphics, for a significant geographical feature or region. (7)

Tracer

Trace the development, history, or evolution of a common or not-so-common invention (ink pens, personal computers, X-ray machines, etc.). Present your findings in a personal research paper, using the handbook as a guide. (Refer to "Personal research" in the index.) (8)

According to Style

Study the writing in a magazine devoted to science and then write an article in that style. (8)

Careers

First research and then write about a career related to a specific field of science, technology, or electronics. (8)

The Business of Science

Write a letter of inquiry or complaint to an interested party, discussing an important science-related issue. (8)

On-Line

Acquaint yourself with a CD-ROM program related to an important science-related topic. Prepare a review and demonstration of the program. (8)

SOCIAL STUDIES

Fables

Create a modern-day fable teaching a timely and important lesson. (6)

"Good Times" Book

Survey students, teachers, cooks, janitors, administrators, and former students for anecdotes (stories) about life in your school. Compile these stories into a booklet. (6)

Do's and Don'ts

Develop a manual explaining classroom rules, the operation of equipment, emergency procedures, and so on for the school. (6)

In and Out of Fashion

Write a feature article about a former or present fad or fashion. (Refer to "Feature, news" in the handbook index for help. Also refer to popular magazines and newspapers for model feature articles.) (6)

Community-Leader Digest

Develop a portfolio for publication, complete with profiles of all the elected or appointed leaders in the community. (7)

For a Good Cause

Promote National Education Week, MADD (Mothers Against Drunk Driving), or another cause by writing letters, designing banners, and creating posters. (7)

Who answers to whom?

Research the workings of city government (or of another governing body) and present your findings in a form understandable to a younger audience. (7)

Up Front . . . and In Person

Think of some aspect of family life, friendships, city life, or the American cultural scene and write about it in a personal essay. (Refer to "Essay, Personal" in the handbook index for writing guidelines.) (7)

Movers and Shakers

Read a biography, an autobiography, or articles about an important social thinker, spiritual or religious leader, humanitarian, or citizens' advocate. (People like Mother Teresa and Ralph Nader come to mind.) Report on your findings in an essay (or paragraph) about this person. (Refer to "Writing, About a person" in the handbook index for writing guidelines.) (7)

Make it your business.

Research the history of a building, company, church, store, or restaurant, and present the findings in a news story or feature article. (8)

In Fiction

Select a serious social or personal issue (prejudice, poverty, dignity, etc.) and write about it in a story, poem, or play. (8)

The Reading/Writing Connection

Read a contemporary novel that explores a significant cultural, social, or personal issue. React to the text in a series of journal entries as you read. Afterward, summarize your feelings about the book and about its treatment of the issue in question. (8)

News Break

Present a morning news show, featuring important school, city, and regional news. Scripts could be read over the public address system or presented on an in-school cable network. (8)

Package one candidate to go!

Select someone you know and respect for a hypothetical political office. Plan this person's campaign strategy, complete with handouts, posters, and advertisements. (8)

Before and Now

Interview a parent or grandparent about his or her experience in school. Compare these experiences to your own in a two-part (before and now) essay. (Refer to "Comparison, Essay" in the handbook index for help.) (8)

■ LANGUAGE ARTS

New and Used Equipment

Design a magazine advertisement for
your handbook,
your tennis shoes,
your school, or
a subject of your own choosing. (6)

You were saying?

Develop a conversation between yourself and a character from one of your favorite books or movies. (Refer to "Dialogue, Writing" in the handbook index for guidelines.) (6)

Very Interesting!

Carefully take note of the action in a popular spot—the cafeteria, a store, a restaurant, a gym, etc. Develop the results of your observations in a report. (Refer to "Observation report" in the handbook index for guidelines.) (6)

Have I got a story for you!

Write the tallest tale you have ever written, exaggerating some activity or event that recently took place in your school. (7)

Great Moments in Sports

Re-create (to the best of your ability) a glorious or not-so-glorious moment in sports. This re-creation could be written as a news story, a diary entry, a letter, a story, or a poem. (7)

A Slice of Americana

Interview an elderly family member, neighbor, or acquaintance about growing up and/or working in an earlier time. Present the results of the interview in a character sketch or biographical essay. (Refer to "Character sketch" and "Biography, Writing a" in the handbook index for guidelines.) (7)

"You Were There" Stories

Write a short story based on a brief human-interest story in the newspaper. (Refer to "Story writing" in the handbook index for guidelines.) (8)

Book of Sayings

Collect favorite sayings from quotation books, literature, newspapers, magazines, and other sources (including family members and friends). Prepare a booklet for publication. (8)

In My Own Way

Make note of your own creative process the next time you develop a story, play, or poem. Present the findings in a brief autobiographical paper. (8)

The Great American Novel

Write the opening pages of your first novel, a novel stemming from your own experiences. (8)

■ MATHEMATICS

Poetically Speaking

Express particularly challenging concepts in acrostic poetry. (Refer to "Title-down poetry" in the handbook index for guidelines.) (6)

Story Problems

Create story problems about concepts discussed in class. Exchange your work with a partner, and solve each other's problems. (6)

On the Outside

Discover how math is used beyond the school walls by interviewing an adult in the workplace. Present the results of your interview to the rest of the class. (6)

In Plain English

"Translate" challenging math concepts into easy-to-understand English so even the most right-brained people can understand them. (7)

Columns of Math

Prepare and distribute a biweekly (or monthly) newsletter discussing a variety of math-related issues. (7)

Speaking of Sports

Compile an accurate and comprehensive manual of sports records and statistics for your school. (8)

Language-Friendly Text

Rewrite a page in your math text so that it presents information in a more helpful manner. (8)

Backed into a Corner

In a notebook or journal, write about a confusing or challenging concept or formula, freely expressing honest thoughts and feelings in the process. Continue doing this until the subject at issue makes better sense. Share your writing with at least one classmate. (8)

A MIXED BAG

What's for supper?

Compile a cookbook of your class's favorite recipes. Distribute or sell the finished product. A potluck dinner featuring many of the recipes could be organized. (6)

How do you get your ideas?

Write a letter to an artist, a musician, or a performer, discussing your thoughts and feelings about his or her work. (Refer to "Letters, Fan letter" and "Letters, Friendly letters" in the handbook index for writing guidelines.) (6)

Field Study

Write a review of a recent field trip, highlighting all of the high points and low points related to the experience. (Refer to "Writing, About experiences" in the handbook index for help.) (6)

A Supersensory Single-Phase Translator

Ask a local business, agency, or institution to identify its newest piece of equipment. Discover the reason for the purchase, how the equipment works, and how it has changed the normal course of doing business. Report your findings in a brief personal research paper. (6)

You are what you eat.

Maintain a diet log or journal for a week, noting everything that you have consumed. Discuss the results of this "field study" in a summary report. (7)

Ms. or Mr. Manners

Develop a 1990's-style book of etiquette for students in your school. Focus on classroom conduct, group skills, lunchroom manners, boy/girl relationships, and so on. (7)

Computers

Complete a cluster with "computers" as the nucleus word. (Refer to "Clustering" in the handbook index for guidelines.) (7)

Study Manuals

Put together a study-skills manual for all areas of the curriculum. (7)

Left or Right of Center

Take note of any left-brain, right-brain, or no-brain things you have done during a particular day. (Refer to "Thinking, Using your brain" in the handbook index for help.) Discuss the results of this "field study" in a summary report. (7)

Synthesizing the Arts

Investigate some aspect of technology and the role it plays in the fields of art and music. Share the results of this investigation in a letter to a friend, family member, teacher, or some other interested individual. (8)

The Arts in Review

Write a review of an art exhibit, a concert, a play, a movie, or any other type of performance. Refer to reviews in newspapers and magazines for models. (8)

It all starts with an image.

Interview an experienced artist, musician, actor, or writer, focusing your questions on the creative process. (Refer to "Thinking, Creatively" in the handbook index for help.) Present the findings of the interview in a news story or feature article. (8)

Sound Off!

Write a pet peeve, an editorial, or an essay, discussing some aspect of school life that really bothers you. (Refer to "Essay, Personal" in the handbook index for guidelines.) (8)

Classroom Strategies

The classroom strategies that follow cover a number of areas often overlooked in contemporary writing programs.

An Overview

Evaluating Student Writing

Two kinds of evaluation interest teachers today: **formative** (evaluating while the student is "forming" the project) and **summative** (evaluating the total outcome, or sum, of the student's effort). Formative evaluation does not result in a grade; summative evaluation does. Some teachers do choose, however, to give students a set number of points during different stages in the formative steps in the writing process.

Formative Evaluation

Formative evaluation is most often used for writing-to-learn activities, prewriting activities, writing in progress, journal entries, and so forth. Four types of formative evaluation are widely used:

- Desk-side conferences
- Scheduled teacher/student conferences
- Written questions and responses
- Peer responses

Note: Make sure your students understand writing as a process. Review "The Writing Process" in the *Write Source 2000* handbook when and if necessary.

Desk-side conferences occur when a teacher stops at a student's desk to ask questions and make responses while students are working. In the early stages of the writing process, responses and questions should be about writing ideas, content, audience, purpose, generating ideas, and getting those ideas on paper. Questions should be open-ended. This gives the writer "space" to talk. When a writer is talking, he is thinking, clarifying, and making decisions. Teachers should not attempt to solve problems for the students, but instead ask questions and suggest possible solutions.

Scheduled student-directed conferences provide opportunities for students to initiate conferences with you. Student/teacher conferences usually take one of three forms:

- Student-directed conference
- PQS conference
- Small-group conference

Student-directed conferences may occur when a student has finished a rough draft or a final draft, has identified a problem or need, wishes to establish new criteria for his or her next project, or wishes to share a breakthrough, a success, a "good thing."

PQS conferences (praise-P, question-Q, and suggest-S) will help you refrain from dominating the conference or overteaching. A typical conference lasts from 3 to 5 minutes. First, offer specific and honest praise. Second, ask an appropriate question (one that relates to the writing stage the student is in and one that prompts student talking). Last, offer one or two suggestions. Conferencing becomes easier the more you practice it.

Small-group conferences may be groups of three to five students who are at the same stage of the writing process or are experiencing the same problem. The goal of a small-group conference is twofold: first, to help students improve their writing and second, to help students develop as evaluators of writing.

Build a portfolio of student revising samples. Include before and after passages. "Label" these samples and put them in a binder so students can refer to it whenever they need help with their writing.

Written questions and responses help a teacher vary her or his evaluating techniques, supplement desk-side conferencing, and provide a lasting record.

Collect works in progress. Write comments similar to those you use in conferences and ask open-ended questions so students can actively seek solutions.

In the editing and proofreading stage you can ask, "Why do you need a comma here?" Students must answer the questions and correct the error. However, with inexperienced writers it is best not to mark all of the errors. Draw a double line to indicate where you stopped marking errors.

Students learn just as much from what they are doing right as they do from what they are doing wrong. Make positive comments! Identify good things!

Peer responses help students become expert responders, but you must train them. You have already begun to do this in both desk-side and scheduled conferences.

Provide some guide sheets or forms for students to use in peer conferences. (See 029 in *Write Source 2000* for an example guide sheet.) It is best if students work in pairs and have a very limited agenda. Always model how to use the form for your entire class. Impose a time limit to keep students on task (15-20 minutes).

One very simple process to use for peer advising is to ask a student to read his or her partner's paper and then generate three questions beginning with *who, what, where, when, why,* or *how*. The questions and paper are returned to the writer who responds to these questions. These questions serve as a starting point for a discussion. You can use more elaborate processes as students become better peer responders. (See pages 86-87 in this guide for ideas. Also see "Group Advising" in *Write Source 2000* for more information.)

Summative Evaluation

Summative evaluation produces a grade and is used for final papers and projects. Once you assign a grade, the student interprets this as a signal that this piece of writing is finished. We want our students to value the learning process as much if not more than the final product, and we want their attention on personal goals, not grades.

However, the day will come when we must assign a grade. Here are some general principles to help you do that:

1. Clearly establish the criteria for each piece of writing or for each student. Limit the criteria so you do not overwhelm the student or yourself. Establishing criteria for each student during a personal conference will allow you to fit the criteria to the student and his or her learning task.
2. Ask students to help you develop the criteria. This can be done in personal conferences or with the whole class. Students readily accept and understand criteria they have helped build.
3. Students must have ample opportunities for formative evaluation before their final product receives a grade. Students deserve points for the work they have done during the writing process.
4. Concern for content, fluency, and fresh ideas should be of primary concern during summative evaluation for young writers. Mechanical correctness will follow fluency. As students gain control of their language, their errors decrease.
5. Students should be involved in the summative evaluation. A form that asks them to circle the best parts of their writing, list the problems they encountered, draw a squiggly line around parts they would work on if they had more time, and offers space to list the suggestions they tried gives students input. In addition to the above information, they should be asked how much time they put into a project and what grade they would give themselves.
6. You will be very familiar with the piece of writing because of the formative evaluations. You may choose one of the systems that follow to establish a grade.

Approaches for Evaluating Writing

Analytic Scales establish the features necessary for a successful piece of writing and attribute point values for each feature. The grade derives from the point total. Many students like this form of evaluation because it is concrete, and it highlights specific strengths and weaknesses in their writing. The emphasis of analytic scales tends, however, to be on the parts rather than the whole.

Holistic Grading evaluates a piece of writing as a whole. The most basic approach to holistic grading is to read the paper rather quickly for a general impression. The paper is graded according to this impression. A reader might also compare a particular piece with a number of pieces already graded, or grade it for the appearance of elements important to that type of writing. Holistic grading helps teachers reward creativity, inventiveness, and overall effect.

Task-Specific Scoring accords a grade based on how well a student has accomplished specific rhetorical tasks. A teacher might, for example, create a scoring checklist or guide for a short fiction writing assignment. This checklist would include those elements that are inherent in this writing form—plot, characterization, point of view, etc. Students must understand the criteria for scoring before they begin their writing. This type of grading addresses specific rather than open-ended writing assignments.

Portfolio Grading gives students an opportunity to choose pieces of writing to be graded. This is a common method of evaluation in writing workshops. Workshop students compile all of their work in a portfolio or folder. Teachers require them to submit a specified number of finished projects for grading each quarter or semester. Students enjoy this method of evaluation because it gives them some control over the evaluation process; teachers like it because it lessens their workload since they don't have to grade everything a student has written.

A Performance System, as described in *Inside Out*, is a quick and simple method of evaluation. If students complete a writing activity and it meets the previously established level of acceptability, they receive the pre-established grade or points for completing the assignment. The student either has completed the activity or he hasn't.

Responding to Student Writing

Responding to Nongraded Writing

(Formative)

- React noncritically with positive, supportive language.
- Use marginal dialogue. Resist writing on or over the student's writing.
- Underline points you wish to highlight, question, or confirm. Never circle, cross out, or otherwise undermine the student's writing.
- Respond whenever possible in the form of questions. Nurture curiosity through your inquiries.
- Encourage risk taking.

Evaluating Graded Writing

(Summative)

- Ask students to submit prewriting and rough drafts with their final drafts.
- Scan final drafts once, focusing on the writing as a whole.
- Reread them, this time evaluating them for their adherence to previously established criteria.
- Make marginal notations as you read the drafts a second time.
- Scan the writing a third and final time. Note the feedback you have given. Write a summary comment on the last page of the student's writing.
- Assign a grade. The grade should be consistent with the criteria previously established.

Peer Evaluation

Young writers learn to write by writing. No one questions that. But their ability to improve as writers increases significantly if they read a lot. Any professional writer would tell your students it is essential that they become avid readers if they seriously want to learn the craft of writing.

They would also tell your students that it is important to become part of a community of writers. Writers need to talk about writing with other writers. They also need to know that someone just like them—a writer writing—is available when they need help. That's why it's important that your student writers share their work throughout the process of writing. They need to feel that they are among writing colleagues—all committed to helping each other improve as writers.

A Community of Writers

The reason some teachers find the workshop approach to writing so effective is that it naturally creates a feeling of comradeship among the writers in the classroom.

The exchange of ideas among fellow writers is especially important once they have produced a first or second draft of their work. Writers generally get so close to their writing, so to speak, that they can't always evaluate it objectively themselves. They need their fellow writers, their peers, to ask questions, make suggestions, and offer encouragement. (Use the following minilesson as a possible starting point for peer editing.)

Peer Editing Minilesson

Give each student three pieces of student writing. Erase all names and number papers. Tell students: "One of these samples is a very good example of student writing. A second is average. A third is poor. Read each paper. Predict which is the best, next best, and weakest. Look at content first. Then look at mechanics."

Ask students for their predictions and then ask them to talk about the strengths and weaknesses they found in each piece of writing. Then tell the students how you would rate these papers and your reasons for doing so.

Types of Evaluating

There generally are three types of evaluation that can go on in a peer conference. There can be a **peer content conference** where student writers share ideas about a piece of writing in progress. The guidelines in "Commenting on Writing" (029) in *Write Source 2000* can be used for these conferences. There can be a **peer editing conference** where student writers help each other with editing a revised draft. See the guidelines listed below for editing conferences. Also refer your students to "Correcting: Preparing the Final Copy" (026) in the handbook. And then there are **peer reaction conferences** where fellow writers actually rate the edited writing. See the general reaction sheet printed on the next page for an example. (Adjust accordingly.)

Peer evaluation does not replace teacher evaluation (although it could). Obviously, you will want to help your students as much as you can as they develop their writing. And you will want to rate their final products along with at least one peer evaluator.

Editing Conference Guidelines

In an **editing conference** you should:

1. Sit next to the author so that both of you can see the piece of writing.
2. Read the piece of writing back to the author *exactly* as it is written (mistakes and all).
3. Allow the author to stop your reading at any time in order to edit his piece.
4. When the reading is finished and the author has completed his or her corrections, use a highlighting pen to point out other problem words, grammatical errors, or punctuation problems.
5. Sign your name in the upper left-hand corner of the author's first page so that the teacher will know that you helped edit the piece.

Peer Evaluation: Rating Criteria and Sample Reaction Sheet

General Rating Criteria

4 = Excellent
- clear, smooth-reading sentences
- descriptive details
- correct mechanics
- imaginative
- appropriate word choice
- effective paragraphing (uses transitions)
- recognizable focus
- good organization

3 = Good
- recognizable focus
- good transitions
- few mechanical problems
- clear sentences
- some details and creativity
- well organized

2 = Fair
- lack of organization
- partial development of topic
- usually complete sentences
- mechanical errors that interfere with reading
- faulty paragraphing

1 = Poor
- little or no organization
- underdeveloped topic
- many mechanical errors
- hard to follow

0 = Unacceptable
- little or no effort
- nearly impossible to read
- no focus on topic
- blank page

REACTING AND REVISING SHEET

EVALUATE: Use the following checklist to help you review and revise your writing. (Use this same checklist to react to your classmates' work.)

_____ **Organization:** Is the writing organized so that readers can clearly follow the main ideas? Is each paragraph complete and easy to follow?

_____ **Detail:** Are all of the important points supported with specific details? Do all the details provide important information about the subject?

_____ **Style:** Does the writing include effective opening and closing thoughts? Does the writing read smoothly and easily from start to finish?

_____ **Mechanics:** Has proper attention been given to neatness and accuracy? (Consider readability, sentences, spelling, usage, and grammar.)

Additional Comments: (when reacting to a classmate's work)

_____ What do you like best about this writing? (List two things.)

_____ Do you have any suggestions for improvements? (List any of these ideas.)

Using Writing Portfolios

More and more, language arts teachers are making portfolios an important part of their writing programs. Will portfolios work for you? Will they help you and your students assess their writing? Read on and find out.

What is a writing portfolio?

A writing portfolio is a limited collection of a student's writing for evaluation. A portfolio is different from the traditional writing folder. A writing folder (also known as a working folder) contains all of a student's work; a portfolio contains only a student's best efforts.

Why should I ask students to compile writing portfolios?

Having students compile a portfolio makes the whole process of writing so much more meaningful to them. They will more willingly put forth their best efforts as they work on various writing projects, knowing that they are accountable for producing a certain number of finished pieces for publication. They will more thoughtfully approach writing as an involved and recursive process of drafting, sharing, and rewriting, knowing that this process leads to more effective writing. And they will more responsibly craft finished pieces, knowing that their final evaluation will depend on the finished products they include in their portfolios.

How many pieces of writing should be included in a portfolio?

Although you and your students will best be able to decide this, we advise that students compile at least three pieces of writing in a portfolio each quarter. (Students could contract for a certain amount of required writing.) All of the drafts should be included for each piece. Students should also be required to include a reflective writing or self-critique sheet that assesses their writing progress.

Note: Some teachers allow students to include one or two pieces of writing from other disciplines in their portfolios.

When do portfolios work best?

Students need plenty of class time to work on writing if they are going to produce effective portfolios. If they are used right, portfolios turn beginning writers into practicing writers. And practicing writers need regularly scheduled blocks of time to "practice" their craft, to think, talk, and explore options in their writing over and over again. Portfolios are tailor-made for language arts classrooms that operate as writing workshops.

How can I help my students with their portfolio writing?

Allow students to explore topics of genuine interest to them. Also allow them to write for many different purposes and audiences and in many different forms.

In addition, expect students to evaluate their own writing and the writing of their peers as it develops—and help them to do so. (See "Group Advising" in the handbook for help.) Also, provide them with sound guidance when they need help with a writing problem. And create a stimulating classroom environment that encourages students to immerse themselves in writing.

How do I grade a portfolio?

Base each grade on goals you and your students establish at the beginning of the grading period and on what is achieved as evidenced in the portfolio. Many teachers develop a critique sheet for assessment that is based on the goals established by the class. (It's very important that students know how many pieces they should include in their portfolios, how their work should be arranged in their portfolios, how the portfolios will be assessed, and so on.)

> *"Portfolios have become each student's story of who they are as readers and writers, rich with the evidence of what they are able to do and how they are able to do it."*
>
> —LINDA RIEF

What About Grammar?

We do not look at grammar as a traditional course of study in which rules and isolated sentence analysis and diagramming are emphasized. To our way of thinking, grammar study must be closely related to the "real" language of speakers and writers of the standard dialect.

And, we see grammar as best taught in the context of the students' own work. What follows is a list of classroom practices and approaches that promote meaningful context-based grammar instruction.

Promoting Meaningful Grammar Instruction

- Link grammar work as much as possible to the students' own writing.
- Make editing and proofreading of the students' writing an important part of classroom work. Students should have ready access to a resource for their proofreading. ("The Yellow Pages" in *Write Source 2000* will answer any questions students might have.) They should also have practice editing and proofreading cooperatively.
- Discover and investigate. Let students learn about grammar for themselves, logically and deductively. For example, the following scenario lets students discover the relationship between a pronoun and its antecedent.

Step 1: Read this sentence.

The day will begin with a private breakfast where they will meet many of the hospital staff who helped them cope with the disaster.

Step 2: Answer each of the following questions (orally or in writing).

1. Who are "they" and "them"?
2. What noun could you substitute for these pronouns?
3. Why this noun?
4. Write a sentence that could come before the example sentence. (Use the noun in your new sentence.)
5. __________ (the noun) is an antecedent for the pronouns "they" and "them."
6. Define antecedent.

- Use 10- to 15-minute minilessons or workshop activities for grammar instruction. Avoid hour-long grammar activities. (See pages 133-152 in this guide for examples.)
- Make grammar instruction fun as well as instructive. Have students dramatize the parts of speech. Develop grammar games and contests. (See the following page for two ideas.)
- Immerse students in all aspects of language learning: reading, writing, speaking, listening, and thinking. Putting language to good use comes from using language, in all of its forms, on a regular basis.

Approaches to Use

Sentence combining—Use the students' own writing as much as possible. The rationale behind combining ideas and the proper punctuation for combining should be stressed.

Sentence expansion and revising—Give students practice adding and changing information in sentences that they have already created. Also have them expand and revise each other's writing.

Sentence transforming—Students should practice changing sentences from one form to another (from passive to active, beginning a sentence in a different way, using a different form of a particular word, etc.).

Sentence imitation—Students should have practice imitating writing models. According to James Moffett, this activity is a great teacher of grammar because it exposes young writers to the many possibilities of English grammar beyond the basic forms. (See the *Write Source 2000* handbook for guidelines and models.)

Daily Oral Practice

It is possible to teach grammar using new and fun activities. Middle-school students like these two methods.

MUG (Mechanics, Usage, Grammar) Shots

Time: 5-10 minutes. Sustained practice is the key to success.

Purpose: (1) To identify skills students are misusing. (2) To maintain skills.

Materials: Use sentences from student writing; ask students to write sentences full of errors and to contribute sentences they are currently having trouble correcting.

Method: Write two incorrect sentences on the board. Choose one of the following plans:

PLAN 1:

Each student copies the sentences and corrects them. Secondly, conduct an oral correcting session.

PLAN 2:

Ask students to volunteer corrections orally.

It is most important that students attempt to explain the reason for each correction they offer. Classmates and the teacher may help them zero in on the exact reason. An atmosphere of discovery, cooperation, and investigation helps students risk making corrections.

Note: See page 163 in this guide for an explanation of our complete daily language program.

Gramo (a game about the parts of speech)

Time: 10-15 minutes or longer if desired.

Purpose: (1) To teach the parts of speech. (2) To let students discover the complexity (and richness) of our language.

Materials: You will have to make the following: Gramo cards and a teacher's master card. See samples on the next page.

Rules: Just like bingo.

1. Players each have a game card and tabs or markers.
2. The teacher has a master card and something to use for markers (bits of paper will do).
3. The teacher calls out a word ("G bug") and players mark on their cards. ("Bug" can be a noun, verb, or adjective.)
4. On a piece of scratch paper students note which word was called and where they marked their card. For example, G-bug-N or G-bug-V.
5. When a player has filled a row, column, or diagonal with markers, he yells out "Gramo."
6. All players wait for the "Gramo" player to recite his or her answers. (Anyone who thinks they also have a winning card must say "Gramo" before the answers are read aloud.) There can be several winners in one game.
7. If there is a winner (or winners), everyone then clears their card for a new game to begin.
8. If there is no winner (maybe the student who yelled "Gramo" had an incorrect answer), the other players should not clear their cards and that particular game continues until there is a winner.
9. Cards can be traded after a couple of games.
10. Rules can be extended: Play two cards at one time; play four corners.
11. Allow only two wins on one card; then the card must be traded. This keeps top players from monopolizing the game.
12. If a card has "noun" printed in two squares under the same letter ("noun" might be in two squares under the letter "G"), the player may put a marker on each square. This makes that card more valuable.

Giving points keeps students on task and acts as a reward. You or a designated student can place a check after each student's name when he or she offers a correction or wins a round of "Gramo."

GRAMO				
Noun	Noun	Noun	Noun	Noun
Verb	Verb	Verb	Verb	Verb
Adjective	Adjective	Adjective	Adjective	Adjective
Preposition	Preposition	Preposition	Preposition	Preposition
Proper Noun	Proper Noun	Proper Noun	Proper Noun	Proper Noun
Conjunction	Conjunction	Conjunction	Conjunction	Conjunction
Adverb	Adverb	Adverb	Adverb	Adverb
Pronoun	Pronoun	Pronoun	Pronoun	Pronoun

Teacher's Master Card

GRAMO				
ADJ	PREP	ADJ	ADVERB	VERB
VERB	NOUN	ADVERB	PREP	PRONOUN
PRONOUN	ADVERB	FREE SPACE	PRONOUN	NOUN
CONJ	PRONOUN	CONJ	ADJ	ADVERB
NOUN	ADJ	ADVERB	VERB	PREP

Sample Game Card

GRAMO					
			FREE SPACE		

Reading Strategies

The reading strategies on the following pages can serve as a basis for an active, personalized reading program.

Luke Skywalker,
saggy-jeaned and flanneled,
burst into the room,
slapped his well-read space book
on a desktop,
and started talking of Chewbacca,
Princess Lea, and Death Star
to anyone who would listen.
He bubbled with the discoveries he had made.

A Teacher's Guide for Young Readers
Active Reading

Is Luke a typical young reader? We hope so. But maybe that is wishful thinking on our part. We do know for a fact, however, that if you teach in a middle school or junior high you have had at least a few Luke Skywalkers. You know who we are talking about. The young readers who take their books to heart—who get actively involved in their reading with eyes welling or nostrils flaring.

You can accommodate the Luke Skywalkers, and, better yet, spark even your most reluctant readers by promoting ACTIVE READING in your classroom. ACTIVE READING gets students involved. It encourages young readers to read books that are important to them, and it encourages them to explore their thoughts and feelings about their reading. ACTIVE READING not only makes reading enjoyable and meaningful for your students, it develops within them an appreciation for literature.

"The primary subject matter for the reader is the web of feelings, sensations, images, and ideas that he weaves between himself and the text."

—LOUISE ROSENBLATT

What can you do to promote ACTIVE READING?

Start by encouraging your students to express their feelings in your classroom. This may not sound like much, but you have a lot of "unteaching" to do. Your students have been trained from their very first school activities to stick to the facts, to look for right answers. So give them class time to write freely and honestly about their lives. Ask them for their first impressions to various lessons or activities; seek their emotional responses whenever possible. The more practice, the better.

What does this have to do with ACTIVE READING? Once students feel comfortable talking and writing about their feelings in general, the more apt they will be to get personally engaged in the books they are reading. And once that happens, reading becomes much more than schoolwork; it becomes, as reading researcher David Bleich states, "a special opportunity [for students] to engage the emotions and thoughts foremost in their minds." And these opportunities are just what the Luke Skywalkers are looking for, and just what might turn your most reluctant readers on to books.

What else can a teacher do to promote ACTIVE READING?

■ **ACTIVE READERS need access to popular young adult and classic titles.**

This means that you will need a classroom paperback library well stocked with the most popular titles for young readers. And your students should have easy access to these books. There is nothing more frustrating to ACTIVE READERS than a delay in getting into a new book, or, worse yet, being stuck with a book that bores them. Young readers should have the same freedom as adult readers—to exchange books whenever they are ready to move on to a new one. (See page 103 in this guide for a list of popular titles.)

■ **ACTIVE READERS need class time to read.**

At least one full class period per week should be devoted to reading. If students are given an opportunity to get lost in good books in school, they will be more willing to read outside of class as well. ACTIVE READING in class helps promote ACTIVE READING outside of class (and that can mean less time spent in front of the television).

■ **ACTIVE READERS need time to react to their reading.**

Young readers like Luke Skywalker have strong feelings and ideas about their reading that they need to express. They can best do this by keeping a journal while they read. Then, whenever they need to react in some way to their reading, they can explore these feelings in their journals.

You might direct them to write a certain number of entries (at least four or five) for each book. You might also suggest that they write at least one entry after the opening chapter, at least three entries during their reading, and one entry after finishing the book. Middle-school students can easily write entries of a half page or longer in their journals if they are reading books of their own choosing.

If some of your students have trouble making anything but cursory remarks about their reading, encourage them to write entries nonstop. Uninterrupted writing (5-10 minutes per entry) naturally produces a free flow of ideas and helps students get the feel for exploring their thoughts and feelings.

Questions for journal writing are listed on the next page and in "Keeping a Reading-Response Journal" in this guide. Also, see "Journal Writing" in *Write Source 2000* for more writing guidelines.

■ **ACTIVE READERS need feedback to their journal ideas.**

Young readers will appreciate your reaction to their journal entries, during the reading as well as after the reading. Encourage them to submit their entries at any time. This is especially important if they need something clarified during their reading and writing—something that can't wait until the book is completed. This exchange of ideas enhances ACTIVE READING.

You don't have to write long, detailed reactions to a student's entries. Simply show them with sincere comments that you are interested in their ideas.

When you evaluate a reading journal, consider two things. First, consider a student's commitment. That is, ask yourself if a set of journal entries reflects a sincere effort on the part of the writer. Second, consider a student's basic knowledge of the book. Someone who has not read carefully will be hard pressed to produce meaningful journal entries.

■ **ACTIVE READERS need time to share their thoughts and feelings with their classmates.**

Time should be set aside whenever possible for class or group discussions. During one discussion, your students might share favorite journal entries with the class or their reading group. During another discussion, they might raise certain questions about their reading. (This is especially effective if you have a group of students who have read the same book.) At another time, students might review their books (without giving away the entire plot).

How will ACTIVE READING help you as a teacher?

ACTIVE READING will give you insights into your students' understanding and appreciation of literature. These insights will help you tailor your literature-related activities to the specific needs of your classes. Maybe a certain class has trouble identifying the themes (statements about life) in the books they have read. Another class may have trouble judging the strengths and weaknesses of certain books, while another wants to know more about science-fiction books and writers.

ACTIVE READING also offers you an opportunity to challenge your students with stimulating composition assignments. Your ACTIVE READERS will have identified a number of important ideas in their journal writing and discussions that they will want to develop further. Students are much more willing to develop thoughtful writing assignments when they are based on their own discoveries and ideas.

Note: In order for ACTIVE READING to work, you must establish certain guidelines. Students must know that reading time is not free time, but time to read or react to their reading. They must also know that they can't waste reading time by simply picking through your paperback library. Finally, it is important that you serve as a reading role model. Read and react along with your classes (at least at the start of the program) so students realize that you take ACTIVE READING seriously.

Questions for Reading Journals

Use these questions to help your students write in their reading journals. This list is not meant to cover all of the issues that might concern your students as they write, and it should be used only when they need a starting point for a journal entry. Their own thoughts and feelings are always the best source for their writing. (See "Keeping a Reading-Response Journal" in this guide for a more in-depth list of questions.)

1. What were your feelings after reading the opening chapter(s) of this book? After reading half of the book? After finishing it?
2. Did this book make you laugh? Cry? Cringe? Smile? Cheer? Explain your reaction.
3. What connections are there between the book and your own life? Explain.
4. What are the best parts of this book? Why? What are the worst parts of this book? Why?
5. What is the author saying about life and living through this book? Explain.
6. What parts of the book seem most believable? Why? What parts seem unbelievable? Why?
7. Do you like the ending of the book? Why or why not? Do you think there is more to tell? What do you think might happen next?
8. What do you feel is the most important word in the book? The most important passage? The most important element (an event, a character, a feeling, a place, a decision)? Why is it important?
9. In what ways are you like any of the characters? Explain.
10. Do any of the characters remind you of friends, family members, or classmates? Explain.
11. What character would you like to be in this book? Why? What personality traits of this character would you like to acquire? Explain.
12. What would you and your favorite character talk about in your first conversation? Begin the conversation.
13. Do you think the title fits the book? Why or why not?
14. What makes you wonder in this book? Why? What confuses you in this book? Why?
15. What came as a surprise in the book? Why?
16. Has this book helped you in any way? Explain.
17. How have you changed after reading this book? Explain.
18. How do you picture the author of this book? Why do you picture him or her in this way?
19. What questions would you like answered after reading this book?
20. Who else should read this book? Why? Who shouldn't read this book? Why?

Keeping a Reading-Response Journal

While students are "experiencing" a book, they should be encouraged to record their journey in a journal. Set aside class time specifically for journal writing. Students can use the following ideas as starting points for their writing, but encourage them to explore whatever issues they feel are important.

Plot and Character

- Simply "free-write" about the book for 5-10 minutes each day.
- Write a description of the main character after reading the first chapter.
- After reading several chapters (or about half the book), predict what you think will happen.
- Write a short summary of every chapter (or every 10-15 pages if the chapters are long).
- When you are about halfway through the book, list the characters and briefly tell how you feel about each one of them. Do this again when you have completed the book. Did your feelings change?
- What character do you feel closest to after the first chapter? After you're halfway through the book? Why? Is this the same character you feel closest to when the book ends?
- Keep a time line or "chronolog" of events as they happen.
- Write a dialogue between you and one of the characters. What would you ask this character? How would he or she respond?
- How does the main character interact with other people? Do you like the way he or she treats other people?

Setting and Theme

- Write a description, draw a picture, or create a map of the setting(s).
- If your book is set in a particular country or place, jot down sentences that give you an idea of what that place is like. If your book occurs at a particular time in history, can you gather information about that time from this book? If so, make a list of your findings.
- Ask yourself this question: "What is the author trying to tell me in this book?"
- Identify important words or phrases in the book. Explain why they are important.
- Paste into your journal any newspaper or magazine articles you find that relate to the book or its themes in any way. You might want to search for some critiques of this book in the library, make copies, and include them.

Personal Reaction

- Make a list of the many different ways you feel while you read. Uneasy? Fearful? Crushed? Restless? Worried? Hopeful? Annoyed? Peaceful? Free? Sympathetic? Your class or some groups might choose to make a list of all the feelings that seem to be experienced when reading books.
- Record what was happening in the book when you were having a particular feeling. ("I was angry when . . . ")
- Pinpoint where you were in the book when you became so involved you didn't want to quit reading.
- What memories is this book triggering in you? List these memories and choose one or more to describe in greater detail.
- What new thoughts or ideas come to you as you are reading this book? Keep a list.
- Record anything that seems really important to you while you are reading.

Style and Word Choice

- Copy those sentences, quotations, and passages that move you in some way.
- List words from the book that you would like to know and use in your own writing.
- What skill are you working on as a writer? Watch how the author of this book uses that skill. Are you learning to show instead of tell? Copy some sentences or passages that you feel are excellent examples of this skill. Are you learning to write dialogue? How does this author get into and out of dialogue?

Reading-Response Journal Workshop:
A Sample Sequence of Events for the First Week

<table>
<tr><th>Time</th><th>MONDAY</th><th>TUESDAY</th><th>WEDNESDAY</th><th>THURSDAY</th><th>FRIDAY</th></tr>
<tr><td>8:00-
8:15</td><td>Explain response journals and provide students with ideas for responses. (See pages 97-98 in this guide.)</td><td colspan="2" rowspan="2">Independent Reading & Responding</td><td>Read some exit slips to students. Discuss what groups did well and what can make the next sharing session even better.</td><td>Small Group
Share one or two of your journal responses.</td></tr>
<tr><td>8:15-
8:30</td><td>Students choose a book.</td><td>Second Minilesson Group Skills
(See 432-449 in Write Source 2000.)*</td><td>Optional time for groups who are still active. Other groups begin reading independently.</td></tr>
<tr><td>8:30-
8:50</td><td>Silent Reading</td><td>First Minilesson Group Skills
(See 432-449 in Write Source 2000.)*</td><td>Small Group
Tell group members what book you are reading and share one or two of your journal responses.</td><td colspan="2">Independent Reading & Responding</td></tr>
<tr><td>8:50-
8:55</td><td>Write a journal response.</td><td>Pairs may need this time to complete group skill work. Other students may choose journal responses to share.</td><td>Exit Slip
What did my group do well today?</td><td></td><td>Have a nice weekend!</td></tr>
</table>

HOMEWORK: For two or three nights during the week, assign students to read and respond for at least 30 minutes on their own. (Optional.)

*Pair students. One student reads aloud the information about one group skill. The other student listens and retells what he or she has heard. Switch roles for the next group-skills session.

Reading to Learn

Real Questions for Real People

Asking students to search their own experiences when they read brings reading to a deeper personal level—a level where they can engage and share. The information and sample questions that follow should help you and your students make reading more personal.

By searching a text for real-life issues, students will find another avenue to comprehension and appreciation, an opportunity to improve their understanding of the human condition, and a chance to actively pursue "ownership" of their reading.

Two prerequisites for effective use of real-life questions follow:

First: A classroom climate has to be established that promotes expression of real thoughts and feelings. Having your students write and share entries in personal journals will help build the right classroom climate for real-life questions.

Second: Understand that middle-school students are particularly interested in the following areas: friendship, family relationships, peer behavior, coping, relating to individual differences, other cultures, understanding male and female, and adopting personal values.

When your class is ready to tackle real-life questions, the following steps will help you successfully initiate this activity.

Step 1: Give students sample questions. Use the ones we include on the following page or compose your own.

Step 2: Select a short story to read together. Ask students to watch for and note "real" questions while they read. You may choose to collect their questions or ask them to present them orally. The method you use will depend on how "safe" your classroom environment has become.

Step 3a: If you collect questions, you can now compose a discussion question(s) using the student responses.

Step 3b: If you ask students to present their questions orally, select one and begin a whole class discussion.

Step 4: The whole class discussion serves as a model for the small group discussions that will become the norm. Using small groups will give all students more opportunities to participate and provide an atmosphere that promotes risk taking. Some students feel that sharing real feelings and thoughts is risky until they've practiced it awhile.

Step 5: The following day students should participate in small groups after reading another short story. The instructor may create a "real" question for these discussions.

Step 6: Ask students to watch for "real" questions as they read. Whenever they find one, they should write it down and put it in a box designed for this purpose. These contributions are not signed.

Step 7: Designated students (or the instructor) can select questions for discussion that are appropriate for the reading they are doing and will help students make meaning out of their lives.

Sample Questions

1. Was *(name of character)* **obsessed with how she or he looked?**

- Do some age groups seem to be more obsessed with how they look? What age groups are particularly interested in how they look?
- How do you know when someone is obsessed with how he or she looks?
- How do you feel about someone who is obsessed with his or her appearance? How do you feel if this person is someone your own age? Someone who is 40? Someone of another race or culture?

2. Did *(name of character)* **use a brother/sister/someone else as a standard for comparison?**

- Do you often compare yourself with someone?
- Do you personally know the person you use for comparison or is it someone famous?
- Do you compare to make yourself feel better?
- Does your comparison ever make you feel inferior?
- What criteria do you use for comparison?

3. Did *(name of character)* **have a boyfriend/girlfriend?**

- Why do you think they liked each other?
- Did they have any problems staying friends?
- Was coping with sexuality a problem for them?
- Do adults ever seem to have problems coping with sexuality?

4. Did *(name of character)* **have a close relationship with an adult?**

- Was this relationship a positive one?
- How could parents of people your age get close to you in order to help you with difficulties?
- Are you willing to express your thoughts and feelings to adults? To parents? To teachers? Why? Why not?

5. Did *(name of character)* **use shocking language?**

- If yes, why?
- How did the cursing make __________ feel? How do you feel about __________'s choice of words?
- Do you curse? Why? When? Why not?

6. How did *(name of character)* **feel when he or she perceived that** *(name of character)* **disapproved of him or her?**

- How did __________ cope with __________'s disapproval? Rejection?
- How do you feel when you perceive someone disapproves of you or something you are doing?

Evaluating Your Students

When students are asked to give personal opinions and personal reactions to the books they read, it is not possible to grade them. How can you evaluate your students in these situations? You might find the following criteria useful:

1. How much classroom time does a student spend on reading and reacting?
2. What is the intensity or level of his or her concentration?
3. How much enthusiasm does he or she express?
4. What degree of care does the student show?

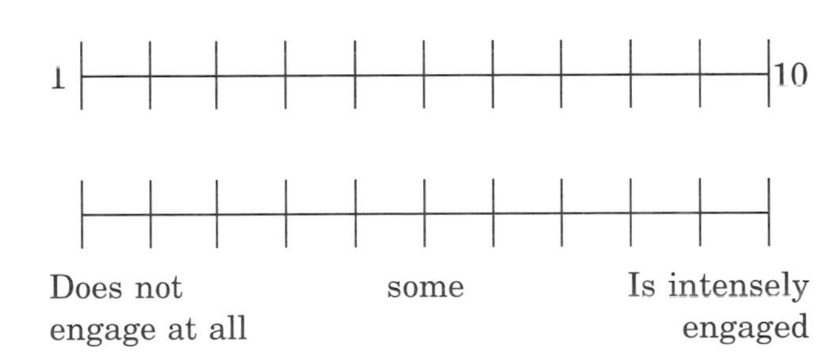

Reading for Pleasure

> *"There has been a conceptual shift in the way many researchers and teachers think about reading that gives students a much more active role in the learning and reading comprehension process."*
>
> —READING REPORT CARD NAEP

Experiencing Literature

We must give students an opportunity to read for pleasure. We must let them lose themselves in a book or other pieces of writing without asking for a response or conducting an evaluation.

We must give them time . . . time to discover all the worlds and feelings and people who live between the covers of books. We must give them time and space to experience reading like Emily Dickinson did . . . "If I read a book and it makes my whole body so cold that no fire can ever warm me, I know *that* is poetry. If I feel physically as if the top of my head were taken off, I know *that* is poetry. These are the only ways I know it. Is there any other way?"

When we set aside a class period or a portion of a period for pleasure reading, we should model for them the pleasure of reading. This is not a time to correct papers or catch up on paperwork from the front office.

Reading for pleasure means we reduce the rules to the bare minimum. We allow students to abandon a book or read two or three books simultaneously. And, we allow them to share their thoughts and feelings about their reading. (See "Active Reading" in this guide for more.)

The following four rules should be all that is required for pleasure reading to work in your classroom.

1. Have book in hand when it is time for pleasure reading to begin.
2. Read for the entire time.
3. No homework is to be worked on.
4. Do not talk or disturb others.

Pleasure Reading in Action

Here are three effective, pleasurable reading activities for you and your students to try.

Many people still love to hear a book read. Once upon a time it was traditional for teachers to read to students for 10 minutes in the morning and after "noon hour," and, believe it or not, they still do. When you read to your students, you are showing them how to give voice to characters, how to let feelings flow, how to interpret a book. When you read aloud to your students, you are giving them something to share and a chance to wonder together. Sharing a book is a pleasurable way for teachers and students to really get to know each other.

It is true you will not be able to evaluate reading for pleasure, but you can be assured that your students are imagining, anticipating, identifying, and empathizing . . . building a zeal for reading.

Brown Bag Reading is also pleasurable. What is it? Give each student a brown bag. They write their name and a subject of keen interest on the outside of the bag. Each student announces his subject to his classmates and then waits to see what will appear in his bag. That is, he waits to see what a classmate or the teacher slips into his bag. It may be merely a quotation or a note telling him or her where to find a magazine article on this subject. It may be a book or an article clipped from a newspaper. It may be a piece of writing by a student who has the same interest and wishes to share some thoughts or a classroom report from another year. Periodically you can have a "reading for pleasure" session where students can discover what is in their "reading bags." Let students change topics when they wish.

Chew! is also pleasurable. What is "Chew!"? It is a very peaceful and pleasurable way to spend a lunch hour. Students arrive with both a lunch to chew and a book to "chew."

We all know reading is a pleasure. Let's do everything we can to be sure our students discover reading for pleasure, too . . . that they discover again or possibly for the first time that reading makes them wonder and sniffle and sigh.

Middle School

Popular Classroom Titles

The titles grouped below are recommended for use in the middle school as classroom library sets. These popular titles can help promote the reading-writing connection by making reading fun and worth writing about. With a little encouragement and direction, students will be eager to explore their thoughts and feelings about these titles in journals and reading notebooks.

GRADE LEVEL 4

- Anastasia Krupnik — Lowry
- Best Christmas Pageant Ever — Robinson
- Borrowers — Norton
- Bunnicula — Howe
- Chocolate Fever — Smith
- 18th Emergency — Byars
- Fat Men From Space — Pinkwater
- Felicia, the Critic — Conford
- Ferret in the Bedroom, Lizards in the Fridge — Wallace
- Fourth Grade Celebrity — Giff
- Frankenstein Moved in on the Fourth Floor — Levy
- Henry and Ribsy — Cleary
- Hot and Cold Summer — Hurwitz
- In the Year of the Boar — Lord
- Just Tell Me When We're Dead! — Clifford
- Misty of Chincoteague — Henry
- Owls in the Family — Mowat
- Ralph S. Mouse — Cleary
- Soup for President — Peck
- Strawberry Girl — Lenski
- Stuart Little — White
- Summer of the Monkeys — Rawls
- Superfudge — Blume
- Tales of a 4th Grade Nothing — Blume

GRADE LEVEL 5

- Anastasia Has the Answers — Lowry
- Are You There, God? It's Me, Margaret — Blume
- Beetles, Lightly Toasted — Naylor
- BFG — Dahl
- Black Pearl — O'Dell
- Borrowers — Norton
- The Cat Ate My Gymsuit — Danziger
- Dicey's Song — Voigt
- Harriet the Spy — Fitzhugh
- Hatchet — Paulsen
- Homesick, My Own Story — Fritz
- Indian in the Cupboard — Banks
- Island of the Blue Dolphins — O'Dell
- James and the Giant Peach — Dahl
- Jelly Belly — Smith
- Kid Power — Pfeffer
- One-Eyed Cat — Fox
- Otis Spofford — Cleary
- Rabbit Hill — Lawson
- Sign of the Beaver — Speare
- Slave Dancer — Fox
- Stranger Came Ashore — Hunter
- Tuck Everlasting — Babbit

GRADE LEVEL 6

- Can You Sue Your Parents for Malpractice? — Danziger
- Cay — Taylor
- Come Sing, Jimmy Jo — Paterson
- Dark Is Rising — Cooper
- Dear Lovey Heart, I Am Desperate — Conford
- Divorce Express — Danziger
- From the Mixed-Up Files of Mrs. Basil E. Frankweiler — Konigsburg
- Gentle Ben — Morey
- Ghost Belonged to Me — Peck
- The Girl Who Wanted a Boy — Zindel
- It's Not the End of the World — Blume
- Lottery Rose — Hunt
- Mary Jane Harper Cried Last Night — Lee
- Night Swimmers — Danziger
- One-Eyed Cat — Fox
- Sixteen: Short Stories by Outstanding Young Adult Writers — Gallo, ed.
- Sixth Grade Sleepover — Blume
- Solitary Blue — Voigt
- Something for Joey — Peck
- Summer Girls, Love Boys and Other Short Stories — Mazer
- Summer to Die — Lowry
- To Break the Silence — Blume
- Trouble With Thirteen — Blume
- The Zucchini Warrior — Korman

GRADE LEVEL 7

- All Creatures Great & Small — Herriot
- Are You in the House Alone? — Peck
- Banner in the Sky — Ullman
- Can You Sue Your Parents for Malpractice? — Danziger
- The Cat Ate My Gymsuit — Danziger
- Dawn: Portrait of a Teenage Runaway — Sorel
- The Day They Came to Arrest the Book — Hentoff
- Deenie — Blume
- Fifteen — Cleary
- Fingers — Sleator
- Friends Till the End — Strasser
- Hold Fast — Major
- Interstellar Pig — Sleator
- It's Not the End of the World — Blume
- Jean and Johnny — Cleary
- The Luckiest Girl — Cleary
- No Promises in the Wind — Hunt
- Pardon Me, You're Stepping on My Eyeball — Zindel
- Rifles for Watie — Keith
- Swiftly Tilting Planet — L'Engle
- There's a Bat in Bunk Five — Danziger
- The Undertaker's Gone Bananas — Zindel

GRADE LEVEL 8

- Alas, Babylon — Frank
- Alive — Read
- The Autobiography of Miss Jane Pittman — Gaines
- The Boy Who Drank Too Much — Green
- Call It Courage — Sperry
- Clan of the Cave Bear — Auel
- Durango Street — Bonham
- Fifteen — Cleary
- Fox Running — Knudson
- Go Ask Alice — Anonymous
- Harry and Hortense at Hormone High — Zindel
- A Hero Ain't Nothin' but a Sandwich — Childress
- Homecoming — Voigt
- Ordinary People — Guest
- Rainbow Jordan — Childress
- Ransom — Duncan
- Rumble Fish — Hinton
- Sister of the Bride — Cleary
- Stranger with My Face — Duncan
- Tunnel Vision — Arrick
- War Between the Pitiful Teachers and the Splendid Kids — Kiegel
- West Side Story — Shulman
- Young Unicorns — L'Engle

GRADE LEVEL 9

- Beyond the Chocolate War — Cormier
- The Bloody Country — Collier
- Circle of Children — MacCracken
- The Contender — Lipsyte
- Dibs in Search of Self — Axline
- Durango Street — Bonham
- Flowers for Algernon — Keyes
- I Am the Cheese — Cormier
- I Never Loved Your Mind — Zindel
- I Never Promised You a Rose Garden — Greenberg
- Lovey: A Very Special Child — MacCracken
- Mr. & Mrs. Bo Jo Jones — Head
- Night — Wiesel
- A Night to Remember — Lord
- The President's Daughter — White
- Rainbow Jordan — Childress
- Something Wicked This Way Comes — Bradbury
- Watership Down — Adams
- The Wave — Rhue
- Wolf Rider — Avi

Thematic Groupings

The titles grouped below lend themselves perfectly to in-depth units of study where students immerse themselves in high-interest themes or topics. These lists will be of special interest if you are involved in theme teaching in your middle school.

Family Relationships

GRADE LEVEL 6

All-of-a-Kind Family Downtown ..... Taylor
And Condors Danced ..... Snyder
Building Blocks ..... Voigt
Charlie Pippin ..... Boyd
Divorce Express ..... Danziger
Dragonwings ..... Yep
Edgar Allan ..... Neufeld
The Endless Steppe ..... Hautzig
Good-bye and Keep Cold ..... Davis
A Hero Ain't Nothin' but a Sandwich ..... Childress
In Summer Light ..... Oneal
It's Not the End of the World ..... Blume
A Jar of Dreams ..... Uchida
Journey to America ..... Levitin
Letters from Philippa ..... Estern
Mom, the Wolfman, and Me ..... Klein
The Moon by Night ..... L'Engle
The Pistachio Prescription ..... Danziger
Popcorn Days &Buttermilk Nights .. Paulsen
A Ring of Endless Light ..... L'Engle
A River Ran Out of Eden ..... Marshall
The Secret of the Indian ..... Banks
Song of the Trees ..... Taylor
Tracker ..... Paulsen

Another Year Older

GRADE LEVEL 7

About David ..... Pfeffer
Anything to Win ..... Miklowitz
Banner in the Sky ..... Ullman
The Butterfly Revolution ..... Butler
Close Enough to Touch ..... Peck
Cracker Jackson ..... Byars
The Crossing ..... Paulsen
The Egypt Game ..... Snyder
Forever Friends ..... Boyd
Friends Till the End ..... Strasser
Good-bye Tomorrow ..... Miklowitz
Henry Reed's Baby-Sitting Service Robertson
Hold Fast ..... Major
Hoops ..... Myers
I Am the Cheese ..... Cormier
I Never Loved Your Mind ..... Zindel
I Want to Keep My Baby ..... Lee
The Island ..... Paulsen
Midnight Hour Encores ..... Brooks
A Night to Remember ..... Lord
Notes for Another Life ..... Bridgers
The Outsiders ..... Hinton
Remembering the Good Times ..... Peck
Tex ..... Hinton
The Year Without Michael ..... Pfeffer

Searching for Answers

GRADE LEVEL 8

Are You in the House Alone? ..... Peck
Brian Piccolo: A Short Season ..... Morris
The Contender ..... Lypsyte
Death Be Not Proud ..... Gunther
Dibs in Search of Self ..... Axline
Dinky Hocker Shoots Smack! ..... Kerr
Flowers for Algernon ..... Keyes
Goodbye, Paper Doll ..... Snyder
A Hero Ain't Nothin' but a Sandwich ..... Childress
Homecoming ..... Voigt
Memory ..... Mahy
My Darling, My Hamburger ..... Zindel
Night Kites ..... Kerr
The Ninth Issue ..... Malmgren
Notes for Another Life ..... Bridgers
Other Side of the Mountain ..... Valens
The Pigman ..... Zindel
Sarah T. ..... Wagner
Say Goodnight, Gracie ..... Deaver
Taming the Star Runner ..... Hinton
Them That Glitter and Them That Don't ..... Greene
Tunnel Vision ..... Arrick

Learning from the Past

GRADE LEVEL 6

After the Dancing Days ..... Rostkowski
Alan and Naomi ..... Levoy
Be Ever Hopeful Hannalee ..... Beatty
The Bloody Country ..... Collier
The Cage ..... Sender
Charley Skedaddle ..... Beatty
Constance ..... Cove
Farewell to Manzanar ..... Houston
Friedrich ..... Richter
A Gathering of Days ..... Blos
Grasshopper Summer ..... Turner
Jump Ship to Freedom ... Collier and Collier
My Brother Sam Is Dead ..... Collier
A Night to Remember ..... Lord
The Night Journey ..... Lasky
Prince and the Pauper ..... Twain
Remembering the Good Times ..... Peck
Rifles for Watie ..... Keith
Sarah Bishop ..... O'Dell
Snow Treasure ..... McSwigan
Summer of My German Soldier ..... Greene
Tuck Everlasting ..... Babbitt
Turn Homeward, Hannalee ..... Beatty
The Upstairs Room ..... Reiss

Future/Fantasy

GRADE LEVEL 7

The Beggar Queen ..... Alexander
The Curse of the Blue Figurine ..... Bellairs
Dandelion Wine ..... Bradbury
The Egypt Game ..... Snyder
The Farthest Shore ..... LeGuin
Freaky Friday ..... Rodgers
Ghost Host ..... Singer
The Girl Who Owned a City ..... Nelson
The High King ..... Alexander
The Kestrel ..... Alexander
Many Waters ..... L'Engle
A String in the Harp ..... Bond
Summer of Fear ..... Duncan
A Swiftly Tilting Planet ..... L'Engle
The Third Eye ..... Duncan
Time Machine ..... Wells
Tombs of Atuan ..... LeGuin
Unicorns in the Rain ..... Cohen
The Voyage of the Dawn Treader ..... Lewis
The War of the Worlds ..... Wells
The White Mountains ..... Christopher
A Wind in the Door ..... L'Engle
Yukon Journey ..... McLaughlin
Z for Zachariah ..... O'Brien

Out of This World

GRADE LEVEL 8

Against Infinity ..... Benford
Anthem ..... Rand
Beauty ..... McKinley
Born into Light ..... Jacobs
Childhood's End ..... Clarke
Dragon's Blood ..... Yolen
The El Dorado Adventure ..... Alexander
Eva ..... Dickinson
Fantastic Voyage ..... Asimov
Farmer in the Sky ..... Heinlein
The Hobbit ..... Tolkien
Illustrated Man ..... Bradbury
The Illyrian Adventure ..... Alexander
Interstellar Pig ..... Sleator
Martian Chronicles ..... Bradbury
On the Beach ..... Shute
Saturday the Twelfth of October ..... Mazer
The Singers of Time ..... Pohl & Williamson
Singularity ..... Sleator
Star Wars ..... Lucas
Tehanu ..... LeGuin
2001: A Space Odyssey ..... Clarke
Unicorns in the Rain ..... Cohen
Westmark ..... Alexander
A Wizard of Earthsea ..... LeGuin

Multicultural Groupings

To help you and your students celebrate our rich multicultural heritage, we have also grouped important titles spanning our cultural spectrum. High-interest African-American, Asian-American, Hispanic-American, Jewish-American, and Native American titles are included. Use these lists to help you build a multicultural library in your classroom.

GRADE LEVEL 5

About the B'nai Bagels . . . . Konigsburg
All-of-a-Kind Family Downtown . . . . . . Taylor
Amos Fortune: Free Man . . . . Yates
Bright Shadow . . . . Thomas
The Buffalo Knife . . . . Steele
Drift . . . . Mayne
Fast Sam, Cool Clyde, and Stuff . . . . . . Myers
Felita . . . . Mohr
In the Year of the Boar and Jackie Robinson . . . . Lord
Ishi, Last of His Tribe . . . . Kroeber
A Jar of Dreams . . . . Uchida
Jesse Jackson: A Biography . . . . . McKissack
Journey to America . . . . Levitin
Journey to Jo'burg . . . . Naidoo
The Lucky Stone . . . . Clifton
Martin Luther King: Peaceful Warrior . . . . Clayton
Racing the Sun . . . . Pitts
The Secret of Gumbo Grove . . . . Tate
Song of the Trees . . . . Taylor
The Story of George Washington Carver . . . . Moore
The Story of Junipero Serra: Brave Adventurer . . . . White
The Story of Roberto Clemente: All-Star Hero . . . . O'Connor
The Story of Sacajewea, Guide to Lewis & Clark . . . . Rowland
Who Is Carrie? . . . . Collier & Collier

GRADE LEVEL 6

And Now Miguel . . . . Kumgold
The Cay . . . . Taylor
The Defenders . . . . McGovern
Dragonwings . . . . Yep
Escape to Freedom . . . . Davis
Going Home . . . . Mohr
Julie of the Wolves . . . . George
Jump Ship to Freedom . . . . . Collier & Collier
Listen Children . . . . Strickland, ed.
Ludie's Song . . . . Herlihy
Mary McLeod Bethune: Voice of Black Hope . . . . Meltzer
Moccasin Trail . . . . McGraw
My Name Is Not Angelica . . . . O'Dell
Roll of Thunder, Hear My Cry . . . . Taylor
Sadako and the Thousand Paper Cranes . . . . Coerr
The Sign of the Beaver . . . . Speare
Sing Down the Moon . . . . O'Dell
The Slave Dancer . . . . Fox
So Far From the Bamboo Grove . . . . Watkins
Sounder . . . . Armstrong
Sweet Whispers, Brother Rush . . . . Hamilton
A Way of His Own . . . . Dyer
Words by Heart . . . . Sebestyen

GRADE LEVEL 7

The Acorn People . . . . Jones
The Crossing . . . . Paulsen
Crystal . . . . Myers
Dogsong . . . . Paulsen
Edgar Allan . . . . Neufeld
Forbidden City - A Novel of Modern China . . . . Bell
Friedrich . . . . Richter
The Friends . . . . Guy
The Friendship & The Gold Cadillac . . Taylor
The Golden Pasture . . . . Thomas
Harriet Tubman: Conductor on the Underground Railroad . . . . Pety
A Hero Ain't Nothin' but a Sandwich . . . . Childress
Jump Ship to Freedom . . . . Collier & Collier
The Light in the Forest . . . . Richter
Lilies of the Field . . . . Barrett
Listen for the Fig Tree . . . . Mathis
Motown and Didi . . . . Myers
The Owl's Song . . . . Hale
Shadow of a Bull . . . . Wojciechowska
Sign of the Chrysanthemum . . . . . . Paterson
The Slave Dancer . . . . Fox
The Upstairs Room . . . . Reiss

GRADE LEVEL 8

Anne Frank: the Diary of a Young Girl . . . . Frank
Blue Tights . . . . Williams-Garcia
The Cage . . . . Sender
Carlota . . . . O'Dell
Chernowitz! . . . . Arrick
Child of the Owl . . . . Yep
Durango Street . . . . Bonham
The Education of Little Tree . . . . Carter
Farewell to Manzanar . . . . Houston
The Honorable Prison . . . . de Jenkins
I Heard the Owl Call My Name . . . . . Craven
Kim/ Kimi . . . . Irwin
Long Journey Home . . . . Lester
Narrative of the Life of Frederick Douglass . . . . Douglass
The Outside Shot . . . . Myers
Rainbow Jordan . . . . Childress
A Thief in the Village: And Other Stories of Jamaica . . . . Berry
This Strange New Feeling . . . . Lester
Up From Slavery . . . . Washington
Waiting for the Rain . . . . Gordon
Walkabout . . . . Marshall
Young Fu of the Upper Yangtze . . . . . . Lewis

"Read the best books first, or you may not have a chance to read them at all."
—THOREAU

Learning and Thinking Strategies

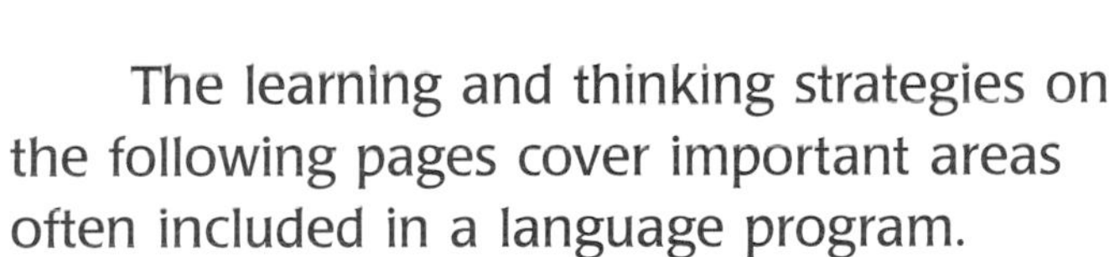

The learning and thinking strategies on the following pages cover important areas often included in a language program.

Active Learning

What can you do to promote active learning in your classroom?

There are any number of active learning approaches that you can work rather easily into your own classroom. Each one of them requires that you slightly modify your teaching to make it more student directed. Some of the most effective approaches are listed below:

(Each one of the following approaches can be used with *Write Source 2000* to promote active learning.)

- **Writing to Learn** (See page 31 in this guide and topics 006-010 in *Write Source 2000.*)
- **Minilessons** (See pages 133-152 in this guide.)
- **Whole Language** (See pages 64-65 in this guide.)
- **Personal Learning** (See personalized writing and learning ideas in *Write Source 2000.*)
- **Creative Thinking** (See pages 116-117 in this guide.)
- **Cooperative Learning** (See 432-449 in *Write Source 2000.*)
- **Make a Writing and Reading Workshop Out of Your Classroom** (See pages 67-68 and 99 in this guide.)

Active Learning . . .

- student plays active role
- student uses original sources and firsthand experiences, in addition to books
- every student becomes a source of information
- questions encourage students' attitudes, ideas, and beliefs
- questions require an answer, not a right answer
- variation in answers is expected
- more and higher-level thinking is required
- leads to appreciation of learning and builds desire to acquire and apply knowledge
- lets students develop how-to-learn strategies that will serve them for a lifetime
- builds self-esteem

Passive Learning . . .

- student plays passive role (sits quietly and listens)
- the text is THE source
- student uses text for nearly all "learning"
- nearly all questions require the right answer
- learning requires mainly lower-level thinking skills
- limits personal and imaginative thinking
- does not allow students to build how-to-learn strategies
- does nothing to build a student's self-esteem

Lots of Questions – A Few Answers

Writing to Learn . . .

Q. What exactly is "writing to learn"?

A. Writing to learn is a method of learning that helps students get more out of their course material. It is thinking on paper—thinking to discover connections, describe processes, express emerging understandings, raise questions, and find answers. It is a method that students can use in all subjects at all ages.

Q. What is the purpose of writing to learn?

A. The main purpose is better thinking and learning. (Better writing is a by-product.) This is why writing to learn is not just for English teachers.

Q. What makes writing to learn work?

A. Writing is uniquely suited to foster abstract thinking. The linearity of writing—one word after another—leads to more coherent and sustained thought than simply thinking or speaking. Also, when writing is used, all students can respond, including those who are reluctant to answer out loud.

Q. What are the advantages of writing to learn for students?

A. Writing to learn provides students with a way of learning, not just a set of facts. It forces students to personalize—to internalize—learning so that they understand better and remember longer. It also encourages higher-level thinking skills.

Q. What are the advantages for teachers?

A. Teachers using writing to learn will see learning, thinking, and writing improve among their students. They will also notice improved communication, rapport, and motivation as students become more independent and more actively involved in the learning process. Also, teachers will come to rely less and less on "writing to show learning," which needs to be graded.

Q. How do you go about beginning a writing-to-learn program?

A. First of all, there is no one "program" for writing to learn. Teachers can begin with the chapter "Writing to Learn" in *Write Source 2000*. After reading, writing, and discussing your way through this chapter, both students and teachers should have a good idea of what writing to learn is all about.

Then the teacher must select, from the wide variety of activities available, those that best suit the needs of her or his students. Once an activity is selected, it is very important that students understand they are "writing to learn," not "writing to show learning." If they understand that they are not writing simply to please their teacher, but to personalize and better understand information, you are on your way.

Q. Which writing-to-learn activities are good to begin with?

A. Learning logs, stop 'n' write, and admit slips (or exit slips) are excellent activities to begin a writing-to-learn program, although any of those listed on the next three pages will work just as well when matched to the right situation.

Writing-to-Learn Framework

PERSONAL WRITING	
Recording	Learning Logs Class Minutes Active Note Taking
Gathering	Brainstorming First Thoughts Listing
Remembering	Focused Writings
SUBJECT WRITING	
Describing	Observation Reports
Reporting	5 W's and H
Corresponding	Admit/Exit Slips Correspondence Unsent Letters
Informing	Student Teachers How-To Writing
Searching and Researching	Summing Up
CREATIVE WRITING	
Translating	Bio-Poem
Inventing	Creative Definitions
Scripting	Dialogues Dramatic Scenarios
REFLECTIVE WRITING	
Reviewing	Writing Groups
Analyzing	Instant Versions Stop 'n' Write Question of the Day

Writing-to-Learn Activities

The following activities can be used to promote writing to learn. Teachers (and students) should experiment with a variety of activities and then decide which ones best suit a particular course.

Active note taking: Students are asked to divide a page in half. On the left side, they are to record notes from their reading, and on the right side, they are to write comments or questions about the material they have read. This written dialogue makes note taking much more meaningful and provides students with material for class discussion.

Admit slips: Admit slips are brief pieces of writing (usually fit on half sheets of paper) that can be collected as "admission" to class. The teacher can read several aloud (without naming the writer) to help students focus on the day's lesson. Admit slips can be a summary of last night's reading, questions about class material, requests for teachers to review a particular point, or anything else students may have on their minds.

Bio-poems: Bio-poems enable students to synthesize learning because they must select precise language to fit into this form. (*Note:* Even though the bio-poem is set up to describe "characters," it can also be used to describe complex terms or concepts such as photosynthesis, inflation, etc.) Bio-poems encourage metaphorical and other higher-level thinking. A bio-poem follows this pattern:

Line 1. First name
Line 2. Four traits that describe the character
Line 3. Relative ("brother," "sister," etc.) of ________
Line 4. Lover of ________ (list three things)
Line 5. Who feels ________ (three things)
Line 6. Who needs ________ (three things)
Line 7. Who fears ________ (three things)
Line 8. Who gives ________ (three things)
Line 9. Who would like to see ________ (three things)
Line 10. Resident of ________
Line 11. Last name

More Writing-to-Learn Activities

Brainstorming: Brainstorming *(list storming)* is writing done for the purpose of collecting as many ideas as possible on a particular topic. Students will come away with a variety of approaches that might be used to further develop a writing or discussion topic. In brainstorming, everything is written down, even if it seems at the time to be a weak or somewhat irrelevant idea.

Class minutes: One student is selected each day to keep minutes of the class lesson (including questions and comments) to be written up for the following class. That student can either read or distribute copies of the minutes at the start of the next class. Reading and correcting these minutes can serve as an excellent review, as well as a good listening exercise.

Clustering: Clustering is a special form of writing to learn that begins by placing a key word (nucleus word) in the center of the page. For example, suppose students were to write a paper on "responsibility" and what it means to them. *Responsibility* or *duty* would be an obvious nucleus word. Students would then record words that come to mind when they think of this word. They should record every word, circle it, and draw a line connecting it to the closest related word. (See the cluster example 035 in the handbook.)

Completions: By completing an open-ended sentence (that the teacher or other students provide) in as many ways as possible, students are pushed to look at a subject in many different ways. Writing completions also helps students focus their thinking on a particular lesson or concept.

Correspondence: One of the most valuable benefits of writing to learn is that it provides many opportunities for students to communicate with their teachers, often in a sincere, anonymous way. If no writing-to-learn activity seems to bring about this kind of open communication, teachers should set up a channel (suggestion box, mailbox, special reply notes, etc.) that encourages students to communicate freely and honestly.

Creative definitions: As in the game "Fictionary," students are asked to write out definitions for new words. Other students are then asked to figure out whether the definition is fact or fiction. When students are given the actual definition, there is a much better chance they will remember it.

Dialogues: Students create an imaginary dialogue between themselves and a character (a public or historical figure, for example) or between two characters. The dialogue will bring to life much of the information being studied about the life or times of the subject.

Dramatic scenarios: Writers are projected into a unit of study and asked to develop a scenario (plot) that can be played out in writing. If the unit is World War II, for example, students might put themselves in President Truman's shoes the day before he decided to drop the atomic bomb on Hiroshima, and create a scenario of what they think this dramatic time in history may have been like.

Exit slips: Students are asked to write a short piece at the end of class in which they summarize, evaluate, or question something about the day's lesson. Students must turn in their exit slips in order to leave the classroom. Teachers can use the exit slips as a way of assessing the success of the lesson and deciding what needs to be reviewed before going on with the next lesson.

First thoughts: Students write or list their immediate impressions (or what they already know) about a topic they are preparing to study. These writings will help students focus on the task at hand, and they will serve as a point of reference to measure learning.

Focused writings: Writers are asked to concentrate on a single topic (or one particular aspect of a topic) and write nonstop for a certain amount of time. Like brainstorming, focused writing allows students to see how much they have to say on a particular topic, as well as how they might go about saying it.

How-to writing: Students are asked to write instructions or directions on how to perform a certain task. This will help students both clarify and remember. Ideally, students would then be able to test their writing on someone who does not already know how the task is performed.

Instant versions: Students are given a composition assignment about a certain subject and then asked to pretend they are actually composing a final draft long before they are ready. Writing instant versions can help students clarify ideas and focus on "the big picture," as well as discover how much they know (or don't know) about the subject being studied.

Journals: Journals are places for students to keep their personal writings, including any of the writing-to-learn activities in this list. Often called "learning logs," journals allow students to record their impressions, questions, comments, discoveries, etc., about any subject, including the positive review given below by a student. (See "Journal Writing" in *Write Source 2000*.)

> *"This journal has got to be the best thing that's hit this chemistry class. For once the teacher has direct communication with every member of the class. . . . Thank you very much for all the help this journal has been to me."*

Learning logs: A learning log is a journal (notebook) in which students keep their notes, thoughts, and personal reactions to the subject. (See pages 52-53 in this guide; also see "Guidelines for Keeping a Learning Log" in *Write Source 2000*.)

Listing: Freely listing ideas as they come to mind is another effective writing-to-learn activity. Students can begin with any idea related to the subject and simply list all the thoughts and details that come to mind. Listing can be very useful as a quick review or progress check.

Observation reports: The classic observation report has long been a staple in science labs. The objective is to collect data from close observation of objects, processes, and events. It is important to remember, however, that as with any writing-to-learn activity, an observation report should be written in language that allows students to personalize or internalize the information being written about.

Predicting: Students are stopped at a key point in a lesson and asked to write what they think will happen next. This works especially well with lessons that have a strong cause and effect relationship.

Question of the day: Writers are asked to respond to a question (often a "What if . . . ?" or "Why?") that is important to a clear understanding of the lesson or that prompts students to think beyond the obvious.

Stop 'n' write: At any point in a class discussion, students can be asked to stop and write. This will allow students a chance to evaluate their understanding of the topic, to reflect on what has been said, and to question anything that may be bothering them. These writings also help teachers assess how the lesson is progressing. (See "Predicting" above.)

Student teachers: An excellent way to encourage students to personalize or internalize class material is to have them construct their own mathematics word problems, science experiments, and discussion questions (which can be used for reviewing or testing). This is a great way to replace routine end-of-the-chapter or workbook questions with questions that students actually wonder about or feel are worth knowing.

Summing up: Students are asked to sum up what was covered in a particular lesson by writing about its importance, a possible result, a next step, or a general impression left with them.

Unsent letters: Letters can be written to any person on any topic related to the subject being studied. Unsent letters allow students to become personally involved with the subject matter and enable them to write about what they know (or don't know) to someone else, imagined or real.

Warm-ups: Students can be asked to write for the first 5 or 10 minutes of class. The writing can be a question of the day, a free writing, a focused writing, or any other writing-to-learn activity that is appropriate. Warm-ups not only help students focus on the lesson at hand, but also give them a routine that helps break social contact at the beginning of each class.

For All Curriculums
Collaborative Learning

Collaborative (cooperative) learning is a powerful classroom strategy for both teachers and students. Collaborative learning is working together like we have always tried to do, but with new knowledge about group dynamics, borrowed largely from the areas of communication and psychology.

Obviously, you already know a lot about cooperative learning. You have been or are a member of many groups—families, sport teams, community groups, faculty committees, and so forth. Sometimes when we look at these groups, we tend to remember how ineffective they can be. It might be we feel we have a large body of knowledge about what NOT to do. This is okay. If nothing else, this is an incentive toward discovering what TO DO.

So what should a teacher who wants to use collaborative learning do?

First, we suggest that you experiment with collaborative learning before deciding if this classroom strategy is for you and your students. We provide three strategies you can use for this experimentation. The group skills you will want to work with are described in *Write Source 2000* (432-449).

While you are experimenting, keep these points in mind:

1. Collaborative learning allows teachers to move away from the front of the room and rely less on lecturing.
2. Collaborative learning provides students with one of the most powerful ways to learn—verbalization.
3. Collaborative learning gives students more ownership of their learning and therefore motivates them to become better students.

Three Strategies That Work

The three strategies you can use for experimentation follow:

1. Tell/Retell Groups

Application: Any reading-to-learn activity

Recommended group size: 2 (3 in one group if you have an uneven number of students)

Group skills to emphasize: Listen actively (433), listen accurately (434), and offer words of encouragement (438).

Step 1: One member reads a portion of the assigned material; the second member becomes an "active listener."

Step 2: The second member tells what she or he heard; the first member becomes the "active listener." They decide together what the essential information is. (It's okay for them to look back at the reading material.)

Step 3: Reverse roles and read the next portion.

2. Smart Groups

Application: Any reading-to-learn activity

Recommended group size: 2

Group skills to emphasize: Request help or clarification when needed (448), offer to explain or clarify (447), and never use put-downs (440).

Step 1: Both students read assigned material. While reading, they put a faint check mark beside each paragraph they understand and a question mark beside any sentence, word, or paragraph they do not completely understand.

Step 2: At each question mark, team members ask for help and clarification. If they both have questions, they try together to make sense of the material. If they both agree to seek outside help, they may consult another team or the teacher. If time allows, they may share what they remember about the passages they both understand.

3. Up with Your Head Groups

Application: Checking comprehension and reviewing

Recommended group size: 4-5

Group skills to emphasize: Help a group reach a decision (449), learn how to disagree (444), and learn from disagreements (445).

Step 1: Ask each student to number off within each group.

Step 2: The teacher or a panel of students asks a question about the material that has been read.

Step 3: Each group "puts their heads together" to make sure every member in their group knows an/the answer. When the question is an "open" question (one without a "correct" answer), the group reaches a consensus of opinion.

Step 4: The questioner calls a number (1, 2, 3, 4, 5) and students with the corresponding number raise their hands to respond. When the question requires a specific answer, only one student need reply; but when the question is "open," a member from each group may reply.

What's the Next Step?

You will probably have many questions after experimenting. Questions such as these are common: "What is the teacher doing while students work?" "How do I assess student work?" "What happens when one group finishes before others?" "What is the best way to form groups?" "Are there more ways to use cooperative learning?" "How can I use cooperative learning in reading workshops? in writing workshops? to build vocabulary?"

Many valuable sources of information about collaborative learning are available to you. Ask other teachers, your curriculum director, and your department head to help you locate these sources. Also check with local colleges. Let your need be known.

Group Skills You Already Know

1. Move desks quietly.
2. Stay in your own space.
3. Sit so all members of a team can see everyone's face.
4. Take turns.
5. Call classmates by their names.
6. Use #3 voices.
   (A #1 voice would be a whisper; a #10 voice would be a scream.)

Teaching Thinking in the '90s

For those of you who are ready to make your classrooms more "thinking oriented," we feel Arthur L. Costa offers the best advice in *Developing Minds* (ASCD, 1985). He suggests teachers teach ***for thinking, about thinking,*** and ***of thinking.***

Teaching for Thinking

How can you create a thinking climate in your classroom? Read on and find out.

- Personalize the learning in your classroom. Students will approach learning more thoughtfully when the subject matter means something to them personally. Common sense (plus plenty of studies) tells us students won't become thoughtfully involved in work that is not relevant to them personally.
- Promote activities that have been considered fillers: stories, poems, posters, letters, recipes, riddles, debates, discussions, etc. These are the types of activities that get students actively thinking and learning.
- Engage your students in projects. Have them produce a class newspaper or magazine. Have them write and produce a play, a news show. Have them develop instructional manuals for skateboarding or bike repairing.
- Involve students in collaborative learning. Collaboration is at the heart of learning outside of school. We learn how to ride, fish, bake, fix, etc., with the help of friends and family members.
- Encourage open-ended, active learning in your classroom. Give students every opportunity to explore, take risks, and make mistakes in your classroom. Ask them open-ended questions. Initiate role-playing activities, dramatic scenarios, discussions, and debates. Pose problems, search for alternatives, test hypotheses, and, generally, challenge your students to think and act for themselves.

Teaching About Thinking

Experts believe it's important that teachers help students think about their own thinking (metacognition). Focusing on one's thinking process leads to better thinking and learning. Here are some things you can do to help students metacogitate.

- Explore with students how the brain works. Discuss left-brain thinking versus right-brain thinking. (See "Using Your Brain" in *Write Source 2000* for help.) Consider a discussion of artificial intelligence as well.
- Select biographies of famous thinkers to share with your students.
- Discuss with your students creative thinking, logical thinking, the connection between thinking and writing, the characteristics of effective thinkers, etc. (See the thinking section in *Write Source 2000* for help with this.)
- Help students think about their own learning. Have them estimate how long an assignment will take. Have them determine what materials they will need to complete an assignment. Have them keep track of their progress during an extended project in a personal journal and so on.
- Remind students that it's all right to make mistakes, to get stuck, to reach dead ends. Help them learn from these experiences.
- Urge students to connect what they have already learned to new information. Also, take every opportunity to connect what they are learning to their personal lives.

> *"Believe all students can think, not just the gifted ones. Let your students know that thinking is a goal. Create the right climate and model it."*
>
> —ARTHUR L. COSTA

Teaching of Thinking

A third component in a thinking classroom includes direct instruction of thinking skills. Here's how to work thinking skills into your curriculum.

- Review a taxonomy of thinking skills, and select a limited number to emphasize throughout the year—perhaps one comprehension skill (summarizing), one analyzing skill (classifying), one synthesizing skill (predicting), and one evaluating skill (persuading). (See 330 in *Write Source 2000* for a list of thinking skills.)
- Produce your own activities for instruction or use thinking materials that are commercially produced. (The *Write Source 2000 Language Program* provides a number of problem-solving scenarios. See the sample below.)
- A thinking-skill lesson plan should follow this general format: Introduce the skill. (Find out what the students already know about it.) Demonstrate the skill. (Get your students actively involved in your "demonstration.") Have your students try this skill in an activity. (Give them an opportunity to work in pairs.) Follow up with a discussion of the activity. That is, have students reflect on the thinking they have done.
- Develop specific thinking activities that complement the "Thinking to Learn" section in *Write Source 2000*. You might
  - ☐ have students identify and work through a problem to solve, an important decision to make, a difficult concept to understand, or an argument to build. (See 308.)
  - ☐ have students refer to the thinking and writing chart (310) regularly for writing assignments.
  - ☐ provide your students with a number of opportunities to focus on specific levels of thinking in writing assignments. (See 311-329.)
  - ☐ give your students opportunities to think and write creatively. (See 331-342.)
  - ☐ give them opportunities to think and write (and speak) logically. (See 343-355.)

Problem-Solving Scenario
INVENTING
Are You Game?

For twenty years Mr. Sporto and his gym classes have batted, blocked, and kicked with gusto. But twenty years is a long time, and Mr. Sporto is losing some of his enthusiasm. What he needs is a new game, a game that will renew the competitive fire in his eyes.

■ **Create a new game or sport for Mr. Sporto, and if it helps him forget football and baseball for a while, he just might use it next semester.** (Work in groups, if your teacher allows it.)

Talking to Learn

Many teachers have proven that talking to learn (verbalizing) is one of the most powerful ways for students to learn. These teachers have been designing and using a variety of effective ways for students to verbalize in classrooms because they know students will comprehend in a lasting way.

Some of the activities teachers have been using are very basic; others are more complex.

Basic Talking-to-Learn Activities

See pages 114-115 in the collaborative learning section for three basic talking-to-learn designs that are appropriate for any content area. After experimenting with these basic talking techniques, students will be better prepared for more talking-to-learn activities in whole class or small group (four to five students) discussions.

More Talking-to-Learn Activities

Nerf Ball Discussion

Instead of merely calling on a student who raises his or her hand, toss a ball. When finished, that student can toss the ball to another student who has raised his hand or back to the teacher.

Talk and Yield Discussion

Use with either a whole class or small groups. The instructor picks the first speaker. When that speaker is finished, he or she picks the next speaker. There are no repeat speakers until everyone has had a turn, UNLESS the speaker who has not spoken volunteers to yield to a previous speaker who wants to make a point.

Read and Speak

Individual students read aloud a piece of writing that impresses them. This may be a page from a novel, a poem, a newspaper article, a scene from a short story or play. You may also have students read sentences or paragraphs from their own writing or another student's writing. After the reading the speaker explains why he or she thinks this piece is worthwhile, exciting, or well-done. Finally, he or she asks for questions from the class.

Using this method with textbooks can be especially effective. Students may choose the data in the text that most interested or surprised them, or they may introduce and read a portion from a piece of supplemental material that is germane to the topic. This could include current magazine and newspaper articles, novels, short stories, poems, letters, and even songs.

Talk and Record Sessions

(For evaluating group discussions)

When it is time for a discussion session, form groups of three to five students. Give each group a tape recorder, discussion guidelines and instructions, and plenty of time to develop their discussions. Upon completion of this group discussion, simply collect the recorded tapes, evaluate the work of each group, and during the next class period, share your observations with the class.

How can the instructor insure a measure of success?

What can you do to make talking to learn work in your classroom?

1. Teach group skills. (See 432-449 in *Write Source 2000*. Require students to practice group skills when they work in groups.
2. Start with one of the basic talking-to-learn patterns. You might use one of these patterns to introduce your students to the information about group skills.
3. Schedule a formal conference with each group whenever a project is lengthy. In formal conferences you can model how talking together can be a productive process. Conferences are also a management tool. You will discover what the group is doing, who is contributing, who is practicing group skills, and what their needs are.
4. Make yourself available for informal sessions with small groups also.

Acting to Learn

At its core, drama is play. It is playful activity in which students use their bodies and senses to imagine people, animals, or objects—in whatever roles they're acting out.

Because drama uses all the performer's senses, it is a useful tool for enhancing learning. The dramatic activities that follow will help your students use multiple senses to learn about literature and language.

> *"Dramatic invention begins in play . . ."*
>
> —JAMES MOFFETT AND BETTY JANE WAGNER

Characterization

Joe Is an Ox—If a student writer has trouble clarifying a character's personality, ask the student to write a metaphor that compares the character to an animal: example—*Joe is an ox*. Ask the writer how ox-like Joe would walk, sit, or speak. Then have the writer watch as other students imitate Joe's bovine behavior by saying pieces of his dialogue, or by doing bits of his action. Encourage the writer to watch and listen for details that may enhance his writing.

Hearing Dialogue—Help writers hear the rhythm of their dialogue by listening to other students read the dialogue. Remind readers to pay attention to a writer's punctuation, sentence structure, and word choice. Encourage writers to consider changing parts that sound unnatural or inconsistent with the characters' personalities.

Listening Games

Ask students to remain seated at their desks and to lean forward, resting their heads.

Relax and Listen—Have students relax and listen carefully. In a quiet voice give these directions: "Close your eyes and breathe deeply, pulling the air from the bottom of your lungs. Let the weight of your body slowly settle on your desk, your chair, and on the floor. When you breathe, breathe deeply. Now listen to the sounds in this room. Identify five . . . five different sounds. [Pause 10 seconds.] Listen to the sounds outside the room . . . identify three. [Pause 10 seconds.] Listen to sounds outside the school . . . try to hear at least one. [Pause 10 seconds.] Now, very slowly, and with your eyes still closed, sit up while I count to 10." Count slowly. When you reach 10, students will be sitting. Ask them to open their eyes and talk about what they heard. (Because the exercise relaxes participants and sharpens their sensual awareness, it works well as a listening activity and as a prewriting activity.)

Listen and Add—Divide the class into groups of 10, and have each group form a circle. Ask a student in each circle to say a simple sentence that ends in a prepositional phrase: example—"I walked here *with my dog*." The person beside the speaker repeats the sentence, but adds an additional object of the preposition: "I walked here with my dog *and Uncle Pete*." The next person may say, "I walked here with my dog, Uncle Pete, *and Donald Duck*." The game continues until someone cannot repeat the list.

Plot Development

Storytelling—To help a writer who gets stuck in the middle of a plot, ask three other students to join in a quick session of storytelling. The writer reads the narrative as far as it goes, and each listener tells what he or she thinks will happen in the rest of the story. Invite the writer to use the ideas to complete the work.

Statues—If a writer cannot resolve the conflict in a scene, play the statue game. Cast the scene. Tell the characters to take their positions described in the scene and freeze like statues. Invite the writer to move the statues' heads, legs, or arms to create the precise picture of the scene. Ask the writer or other students to describe what is happening at this moment, and what might happen next. At this point you may call, "Curtain!" which cues the statues to come alive and improvise the action. Stop the scene as soon as actors lose focus. Invite the writer to use the actors' ideas.

Prewriting Exercises

Concentration—Have students form two lines about six feet apart with each student in one line facing a partner in the other. Instruct line A to turn their backs on line B. Ask people in line B to change three things in their appearance: example— fasten a button, move a ring from one finger to another, and loosen a shoelace. Then ask students in line A to turn around, face their partners, and identify the three changes in the partner's appearance. Repeat the game.

The Storyteller—Have the class sit in a circle, and you stand in the middle. The first person you point to begins a story, "Once upon a time there was a . . ." Snap your fingers as you point to another student. Immediately, this person must continue the story, possibly saying, " . . . huge elephant with bright red ears. Now the elephant hated . . . " Again, snap your fingers while pointing to another student. The object of the game is to continue the story (1) without pausing, (2) without repeating what the previous speaker said, and (3) without changing the logic of the story. Continue the game until the story draws to a natural close. Students learn to concentrate—and they also generate ideas for their writing.

Responding to Literature

Reader's Theater—To help students imagine how characters in a story may look or sound, do a reader's theater performance. Prepare the script by making copies of the story, assigning a narrator to read the narrative parts, and assigning additional readers to read the characters' dialogue. Coach students to use their bodies and voices to suggest the personalities of their characters.

Imitating—Encourage students to assume the personality of a character by imitating how the character would sit, hold a pencil, comb his or her hair, roll up a sleeve, open a door, or say a line of dialogue. This activity helps students imagine characters in professional writing, or in their own writing.

Improvisation—Use improvisation to help students imagine what happens in a short story or novel. Start with a key half-page scene that includes no more than three characters. Read the scene with the class. Then cast the scene, and give the actors 5 minutes to develop an improvisation. Encourage them to act out what happens in the scene, but to improvise their own dialogue. Perform the piece, change details, and perform it again. Ask the class to compare the scene they read with the one they saw.

Pantomime Vocabulary Builder

The purpose of this activity is to build vocabulary and classification powers. Begin with a starter word such as *vehicle, emotion, clothing, machine, gesture, walk,* or *person*, and let the students brainstorm in two to four groups for synonyms for their word. Allow them to use a dictionary or thesaurus if necessary. Supply each group with a separate starter word and small pieces of paper to write down each synonym (a "type" of vehicle, emotion, clothing, etc.). Then, in turn, each group shows one piece of paper to the teacher and pantomimes the word written on it. Perhaps the word is "strut," a synonym for "walk." (The teacher must announce the starter word.) The other groups each have a spokesperson to whom the members give their ideas. In turn, each group's spokesperson guesses the type of walk. If it is correct, that team gets a point. If it is not, another group has an opportunity to guess. If no group guesses correctly, the teacher may award the point to the presenting group, if the synonym was accurately presented, or give no point and tell the word. The second group now begins the process. Other starter words include *country, state, president, food, furniture, occupation, sports, dances, nouns, verbs, adjectives,* and *adverbs*.

Additional Sources:

Improvisation: Learning through Drama. Booth, David, and Charles Lundy. Toronto: Harcourt, 1985.

Teaching Young Playwrights. Chapman, Gerald. Portsmouth: Heinemann-Boynton/Cook, 1991.

Creative Drama for the Classroom Teacher. Heinig, Ruth Beall. Englewood Cliffs: Prentice Hall, 1993.

Creative Drama in the Classroom, 5th ed. McCaslin, Nellie. New York: Longman, 1990.

Student-Centered Language Arts, K-12. Moffett, James, and Betty Jane Wagner Portsmouth: Heinemann-Boynton/Cook, 1992.

Building Vocabulary

We know there is a strong connection between a student's vocabulary and her or his reading ability. The same is true for a student's ability to listen, speak, and write. In fact, we now recognize that each person actually has four vocabularies, one each for reading, listening, speaking, and writing (listed here from largest to smallest). Although there is much overlap, students will always be able to recognize more words than they can produce. This is important to keep in mind as you develop a program of vocabulary development for your students.

Vocabulary development must also occur across the curriculum. Students must read, hear, speak, and write with the words they are attempting to learn in their classes. Anything less, and the words will not become part of their permanent "producing" vocabulary.

Existing studies tell us two things: (1) giving students lists of vocabulary words with little or no context is not an efficient way to teach vocabulary, and (2) students must be actively involved with the words they are attempting to learn.

> *"Colors fade, temples crumble, empires fall, but wise words endure."*
>
> —EDWARD THORNDIKE

Vocabulary-Building Strategies

The vocabulary-building strategies that follow have taken all of these points into consideration:

Previewing in Context

1. Select five or six words from a chapter or selection students are about to read.
2. Tell students to open their books to the page and paragraph in which each word is located. Have them find the word, read it in context, and try to figure out the meaning.
3. Ask students to write down what they think each word means.
4. Discuss possible meanings and arrive at the correct definition in this context.

Context Clues Study

1. Students should read and discuss the context clues section of their *Write Source 2000* handbook.
2. Students should practice identifying the types of context clues as they use the previewing and self-collection techniques.

Self-Collection

1. Students should set aside a portion of their journals or notebooks to collect personal vocabulary.
2. They may collect new and interesting words from any source, preferably outside of school.
3. Students should analyze each word with the help of a dictionary or glossary and perhaps a thesaurus.
4. Students may want to write journal entries that contain these new words.

Vocabulary

word	definition	usage
platonic	a relationship without romance	They had a platonic relationship.

Prefix, Suffix, Root Study

1. Students should learn the most common prefixes, suffixes, and roots.
2. Students can be assigned three or four word parts each week for the entire year (see lists for each level on pages 123).
3. Students can be given a number of strategies for learning these word parts:
   - ☐ Assign students one word part a day (every day except Monday, perhaps). As you are taking roll, students can write out the word part, definition, a sample word, and a sentence using this word. Then have them exchange and correct papers.
   - ☐ Ask students to brainstorm for word associations that will help them remember the meaning of each word part.
   - ☐ Challenge students to combine the word parts they have studied into as many words as possible (perhaps in 5 minute's time, or as an assignment for the next day). Special cards can also be used for this purpose:

Word Card

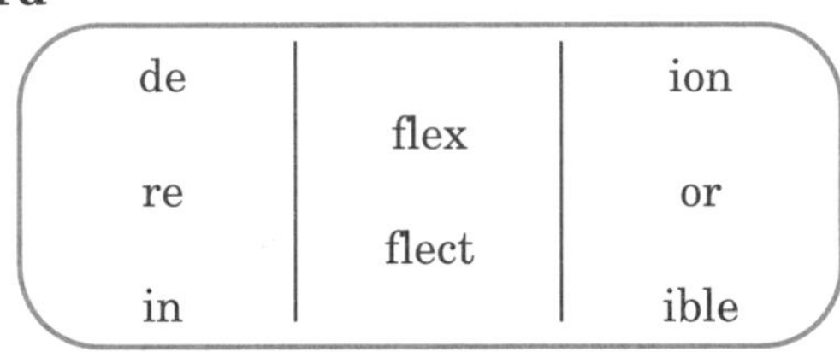

de
re
in
flex
flect
ion
or
ible

   - ☐ Require students to create "new" words, not in the dictionary, using the word parts they have learned. To qualify, a new word should be one that makes sense and might actually be used if it were known to a large number of people.
   - ☐ Invite students to share a "new" word and challenge the others to guess what it means and to write a sentence (or two or three) in which they use this word.
   - ☐ Direct students to start a special section in their notebooks for word parts they come across in their other classes.

Other Forms of Word Study

1. **Special groups.** Students can be introduced to special groups of words found in computer language, music, advertising, politics, etc.
2. **Word play.** A certain amount of "word play" is essential to vocabulary growth. Any type of word game will work so long as it is appropriate for the level of the students.
3. **Word-a-day.** At the beginning of the class period, a word is printed on the board (a word that a student can use in his or her reading, listening, writing, and speaking vocabularies). As students enter the classroom, they immediately grab a dictionary and look up the word. As a class, students discuss the meaning and agree on a definition and a part of speech. They then use the word in a sentence, showing that they know what the word means and how to use it correctly.

   Each student jots down this information in a notebook. Each page is divided by a line drawn vertically at a point about one-third of the width of the page. On the left side of this line, the word is written. On the right side of the line, the part of speech, definition, and sentence are written. This allows the student to cover the definitions by simply folding the paper.

   A written quiz can be given each Friday, covering the five words from the recent week and five words from any past weeks. The student must write the word in a sentence, proving again that he or she knows what the word means and how to use it.

Word Parts Study List

The following lists of word parts can be used as the basis of a vocabulary program for levels 6, 7, and 8.

LEVEL 6

Prefixes: anti (ant), bi (bis, bin), circum (circ), deca, di, ex (e, ec, ef), hemi (demi, semi), hex, il (ir, in, im), in (il, im), intro, mono, multi, non, penta, post, pre, quad, quint, re, self, sub, super (supr), tri, un, uni

Suffixes: able (ible), an (ian), ar (er, or), cide, cule (ling), en, ese, ess, ful, ion (sion, tion), ist, ity (ty), ize, less, ology, ward

Roots: anni (annu, enni), aster (astr), aud (aus), auto (aut), bibl, bio, breve, chrom, chron, cide, cise, cit, clud (clus, claus), corp, crat, cred, cycl (cyclo), dem, dent (dont), derm, dic (dict), domin, dorm, duc (duct), erg, fin, fix, flex (flect), form, fort (forc), fract (frag), geo, graph (gram), here (hes), hydr (hydro, hydra), ject, join (junct), jur (jus), juven, laut (lac, lot, lut), lic (licit), magn, mand, mania, meter, micro, migra, multi (multus), number (numer), omni, ortho, ped (pod), phon, pop, port, prehend, punct, reg (recti), rupt, sci, scrib (script), serv, spec (spect, spic), sphere, tele, tempo, terra, therm, tract (tra), typ, uni, vid (vis), zo

LEVEL 7

Prefixes: ambi (amb), amphi, bene (bon), by, co (con, col, cor, com), contra (counter), dia, dis (dif), eu (ev), extra (extro), fore, homo, inter, mis, ob (of, op, oc), para, per, peri, poly, pro, se, syn (sym, sys, syl), trans (tra), ultra, under, vice

Suffixes: ance (ancy), ate, cian, ish, ism, ive, ly, ment, ness, some, tude

Roots: ag (agi, ig, act), anthrop, arch, aug (auc), cap (cip, cept), capit (capt), carn, cause (cuse, cus), civ, clam (claim), cord (cor, card), cosm, crea, cresc (cret, crease, cru), dura, dynam, equi, fac (fact, fic, fect), fer, fid (fide, feder), gam, gen, gest, grad (gress), grat, grav, hab (habit), hum (human), hypn, jud (judi, judic), leg, lit (liter), log (logo, ology), luc (lum, lus, lun), man, mar (mari, mer), medi, mega, mem, mit (miss), mob (mot, mov), mon, mori (mort, mors), nov, onym, oper, pac, pan, pater (patr), path (pathy), pend (pens, pond), phil, photo, plu (plur, plus), poli, portion, prim (prime), psych, put, salv (salu), sat (satis), scope, sen, sent (sens), sign (signi), sist (sta, stit, stet), solus, solv (solu), spir, spond (spons), string (strict), stru (struct), tact (tang, tag, tig, ting), test, tort (tors), vac, vert (vers), vict (vinc), voc

LEVEL 8

Prefixes: a (an), ab (abs, a), acro, ante, be, cata, cerebro, de, dys, epi, hyper, hypo, infra, intra,macro, mal, meta, miso, neo, oct, paleo, pseudo, retro, sex (sest)

Suffixes: asis (esis, osis), cy, dom, ee, ence (ency), et (ette), ice, ile, ine, ite, oid

Roots: acer (acid, acri), acu, ali (allo, alter), altus, am (amor), belli, calor, caus (caut), cognosc (gnosi), crit, cur (curs), cura, doc, don, dox, end (endo), fall (fals), fila (fili), flu (fluc, fluv), fum, gastro, germ, gloss (glot), glu (glo), greg, helio, hema (hemo), hetero, homo, ignis, later, levis, lith, liver (liber), loc (loco), loqu (locut), lude, matri (matro, matric), monstr (mist), morph, nasc (nat), neur, nom, nomen (nomin), nounce (nunci), nox (noc), pedo, pel (puls), phobia, plac (plais), plenus, pneuma (pneumon), pon (pos, pound), posse (potent), proto, que (qui), quies, ri (ridi, risi), rog (roga), sacr (sanc, secr), sangui, sed (sess, sid), sequ (secu, sue), simil (simul), somnus, soph, sume (sump), ten (tin, tain), tend (tent, tens), tom, tox, trib, tui (tuit, tut), turbo, vale (vali, valu), ven (vent), viv (vita, vivi), vol, volcan (vulcan), vor

Improving Student Spelling

> *"For better or worse, spelling places third in the American public's priorities for curriculum emphasis. Writing places eighth. In short, spelling is more important than what it is used for . . . writing."*
>
> —DONALD GRAVES

How should spelling be addressed in today's language-arts classrooms if, in fact, the public gives it such a high priority? That question and more is explored in this discussion. What you'll find first is a list of instructional do's as reflected in the current research on spelling.

Spelling Practices That Work

- Devoting approximately 10 minutes per day to direct instruction
- Presenting and studying words in short lists
- Drawing words from one of the master lists of high-frequency words
- Employing the pretest-study-test method of instruction
- Asking students to correct their own pretests
- Providing students with a strategy to learn how to spell new words
- Linking spelling instruction, whenever possible, to the students' own writing

Spelling and Writing

There is really only one hard-and-fast rule to remember: Do not let students become overly concerned about the correctness of their spelling during the drafting stages of the writing process. They should, however, be made to realize that before a piece of writing can be considered ready for publication, it must be as free of careless errors as possible.

Meeting Students' Needs

How can you help students improve their spelling skills as they work on their writing? First, you can ask them to circle which words are spelled incorrectly in their work before they ready a draft for publication. If a student needs more direction, you can write at the top of the paper, "There are four words misspelled," and let the student attempt to find the four words.

Next, teach your students the various systems they can use to correct a misspelling. These should include using a poor speller's dictionary, compiling a personal dictionary of frequently misspelled words, utilizing computer spell checkers, and having access to the classroom spelling expert.

Why Spelling?

You may hear from middle-school students, "Why do I have to learn to spell when I can use a computer spell checker?" The truth of the matter is that there is still a very good reason for learning to spell, especially the words a writer uses again and again. A writer who can spell can put the words behind him or her and focus on more important matters like exploring and shaping ideas. Also, once a spell checker identifies a misspelling, a writer still has to know how to correct the error.

Weekly Lists

Weekly spelling words for levels 6, 7, and 8 are provided on the next six pages. These words come from the commonly misspelled words listed at topic numbers 568-573 in the *Write Source 2000* handbook. The "Weekly Spelling Words" can serve as the starting point for planning spelling units. Ten words are provided for each week. Add more words from one of the published high-frequency lists or from units you are studying. (See page 131 in this section for more spelling ideas.)

Weekly Spelling Words: Level 6

1
a-bout
a-bove
ac-ci-dent
ac-com-plish
ac-count
a-cross
a-dapt
ad-dress
ad-mire
ad-ven-ture

2
a-fraid
af-ter-noon
a-gain
ah
aid
a-larm
a-live
al-low-ance
al-to-geth-er
al-ways

3
a-mount
an-gel
an-gry
an-nu-al
an-oth-er
any-body
any-how
any-one
ap-pear-ance
ap-pe-tite

4
ap-prov-al
arc-tic
ar-gu-ment
a-rith-me-tic
a-round
a-sleep
as-sume
at-tach
at-ten-tion
at-trac-tive

5
Au-gust
au-to-mo-bile
av-er-age
bag-gage
bak-ing
ba-nan-a
ban-dage
bar-ber
bas-ket
be-cause

6
be-come
be-gan
be-gin-ning
be-ing
be-long
be-tween
black-board
both-er
bot-tle
break-fast

7
bridge
bright
brought
bub-ble
bud-get
bury
busy
cab-bage
ca-nal
can-dle

8
can-non
can't
card-board
care-less
car-pen-ter
car-rot
catch-er
cat-sup
cel-e-bra-tion
cer-tain

9
chal-lenge
chief
chil-dren
cho-rus
class-mates
climb
coach
col-lege
col-or
com-ing

10
com-mit
com-pan-y
com-par-i-son
com-plain
com-pro-mise
con-cert
con-di-tion
con-nect
con-sti-tu-tion
con-tin-ue

11
control
couldn't
coun-ter
coun-try
court
cous-in
crack-er
crank-y
crum-ble
cup-board

12
cur-rent
cus-tom
dai-ly
dan-ger (-ous)
de-cided
dec-o-rate
de-pot
de-sert
de-sign
des-sert

13
de-ter-mine
di-a-mond
di-a-ry
dis-ap-point
dis-ap-prove
dis-cov-er
dis-cuss
di-vide
di-vine
di-vi-sion

14
dol-lar
du-al
edge
e-di-tion
ei-ther
el-e-phant
el-i-gi-ble
e-mer-gen-cy
em-ploy-ment
en-close

15
e-nor-mous
e-nough
en-ter-tain
en-trance
en-vi-ron-ment
es-cape
es-tab-lish
ex-cel-lent
ex-cept
ex-er-cise

16
ex-pect
ex-plain
fam-i-ly
fa-mous
fash-ion
fea-ture
Feb-ru-ar-y
fif-ty
for-mal (-ly)
forth

Weekly Spelling Words: Level 6

17
for-ty
for-ward
fourth
friend (-ly)
fright-en
gad-get
gen-er-ous
ge-nius
gen-tle
ghost

18
gov-er-nor
gram-mar
grease
grudge
guess
guilt-y
ham-mer
han-dle (d)
hap-pen
hav-ing

19
his-to-ry
hon-or
hop-ping
hos-pi-tal
i-den-ti-cal
im-ag-i-nary
im-ag-ine
im-i-ta-tion
im-mi-grant
im-por-tance

20
im-prove-ment
in-de-pen-dent
in-dus-tri-al
in-flam-ma-ble
in-no-cence
in-no-cent
in-stead
in-tel-li-gence
in-ter-est-ed
in-ves-ti-gate

21
in-vi-ta-tion
jour-nal
jour-ney
kitch-en
knew
la-bel
laugh
le-gal
leg-is-la-ture
length

22
light-ning
like-ly
liv-ing
loaves
los-er
love-ly
mag-a-zine
main-tain
mak-ing
ma-te-ri-al

23
max-i-mum
med-i-cine
mes-sage
min-ute
mir-ror
mis-spell
mon-u-ment
mort-gage
moun-tain
nat-u-ral (-ly)

24
neigh-bor (-hood)
nine-teen
nois-y
o-bey
oc-ca-sion
oc-cur
of-ten
o-mis-sion
o-pin-ion
orig-i-nal

25
pack-age
paid
para-graph
par-tic-i-pate
pas-ture
peo-ple
per-haps
per-son-al (-ly)
piece
pitch-er

26
planned
pre-cise (-ly)
pref-er-a-ble
prep-a-ra-tion
prim-i-tive
pris-on-er
prob-a-bly
pro-fes-sor
pump-kin
pure

27
quar-ter
qui-et
raise
re-al-ly
re-ceive
re-mem-ber
rep-e-ti-tion
rep-re-sen-ta-tive
re-spect-ful-ly
route

28
safe-ty
sal-ad
sand-wich
scene
sci-ence
scream
sea-son
sen-tence
shin-ing
since

29
sol-dier
spe-cif-ic
sprin-kle
stom-ach
stopped
strength
suc-cess
sup-ple-ment
sup-pose
tem-per-a-ture

30
thank-ful
the-ater
thief
though
tired
to-geth-er
touch
to-ward
tried
tries

31
Tues-day
un-til
use-ful
using
va-ca-tion
veg-e-ta-ble
very
view
vis-i-tor
voice

32
weath-er
Wednes-day
wel-come
whale
where
whole
wom-en
worth-while
writ-ing
yel-low

Weekly Spelling Words: Level 7

1
a-board
ab-sent
a-bun-dance
ac-ci-den-tal (-ly)
ac-com-pa-ny
ac-cord-ing
ac-cu-rate
ache
a-cre
ad-di-tion (-al)

2
ad-just (-ment)
ad-ver-tis-ing
af-ter
af-ter-ward
a-gree (-ment)
air-y
a-like
al-ley
al-most
al-ready

3
am-bu-lance
a-mong
an-cient
an-ger
an-i-mal
an-nounce
an-swer
an-tic-i-pate
anx-ious
any-thing

4
any-way
a-piece
ap-par-ent (-ly)
ap-peal
ap-pli-ance
ap-proach
ap-pro-pri-ate
ar-chi-tect
aren't
a-rouse

5
ar-range (-ment)
ar-riv-al
as-sas-sin
as-sis-tance
as-so-ci-ate
ath-lete
at-tack (ed)
at-ten-dance
at-ti-tude
au-thor

6
a-vail-a-ble
aw-ful (-ly)
bal-ance
bank-rupt
base-ment
ba-sis
beau-ty
be-com-ing
be-fore
be-have

7
be-lieve
ben-e-fit (-ed)
bis-cuit
blan-ket
bot-tom
bought
bounce
breath (n.)
breeze
broth-er

8
buck-et
buck-le
build-ing
bur-glar
but-ton
cal-en-dar
can-di-date
can-not
can-yon
cap-tain

9
care-ful
cas-u-al-ty
cat-a-log
cat-er-pil-lar
ceil-ing
cen-tu-ry
cer-tain (-ly)
cham-pi-on
char-ac-ter (-is-tic)
chim-ney

10
choice
class-room
cli-mate
cloth-ing
co-coon
col-lar
col-umn
com-e-dy
com-mer-cial
com-mit-ment

11
com-mu-nity
com-pe-ti-tion
com-plete (-ly)
con-cern-ing
con-crete
con-duc-tor
con-fer-ence
con-scious
con-tro-ver-sy
con-vince

12
cool-ly
cor-po-ra-tion
cough
coun-ty
cour-age
cour-te-sy
cov-er-age
co-zy
crawl
cru-el

13
crumb
cu-ri-ous
cus-tom-er
dair-y
dam-age
de-ceive
de-fense
def-i-ni-tion
de-scribe
de-sir-able

14
de-spair
dic-tio-nary
dif-fer-ent
din-ing
di-rec-tor
dis-ap-pear
dis-cus-sion
dis-sat-is-fied
dis-trib-ute
doc-tor

15
doesn't
dough
du-pli-cate
ea-ger (-ly)
eight
e-lec-tric-i-ty
em-bar-rass
em-pha-size
en-cour-age
e-nough

16
en-tire-ly
en-ve-lope (n.)
equip-ment
es-sen-tial
ev-i-dence
ex-ceed
ex-haust (-ed)
ex-hi-bi-tion
ex-pen-sive
ex-pres-sion

Weekly Spelling Words: Level 7

17
ex-treme (-ly)
fa-mil-iar
fa-vor-ite
fed-er-al
fi-ery
fi-nal-ly
for-ci-ble
for-mer (-ly)
for-tu-nate
foun-tain

18
freight
ful-fill
fur-ther
gen-er-al-ly
ge-og-ra-phy
gnaw
grief
gro-cery
guard
guide

19
hand-ker-chief
hand-some
hap-pi-ness
hast-i-ly
hes-i-tate
hol-i-day
hop-ing
hor-ri-ble
hur-ried-ly
il-lit-er-ate

20
il-lus-trate
im-mense
im-mor-tal
im-pos-si-ble
in-de-pen-dence
in-di-vid-u-al
in-fi-nite
ini-ti-a-tion
in-stal-la-tion
in-stance

21
in-ten-tion
in-ter-est-ing
in-ter-view
ir-ri-gate
is-sue
jeal-ous (-y)
jew-el-ry
knock
la-dies
lan-guage

22
laun-dry
lec-ture
leg-i-ble
li-a-ble
li-brar-y
lis-ten
loose
lose
los-ing
ma-chin-er-y

23
man-u-al
mar-riage
math-e-mat-ics
meant
mea-sure
mile-age
min-i-mum
mis-er-a-ble
mois-ture
mol-e-cule

24
mus-cle
mu-si-cian
nei-ther
niece
nine-ty
nu-cle-ar
ob-sta-cle
oc-ca-sion-al (-ly)
oc-curred
o-mit-ted

25
op-er-ate
op-po-site
par-a-dise
par-al-lel
par-tic-i-pant
par-tic-u-lar (-ly)
pe-cu-liar
per-ma-nent
per-sis-tent
per-spi-ra-tion

26
phase
phy-si-cian
play-wright
pleas-ant
plea-sure
pos-sess
pos-si-ble
prac-ti-cal (-ly)
pre-ferred
pres-ence

27
pre-vi-ous
prin-ci-pal
prin-ci-ple
priv-i-lege
pro-ce-dure
pro-nun-ci-a-tion
pro-tein
quite
re-al-ize
rec-og-nize

28
rec-om-mend
re-lieve
re-li-gious
re-spon-si-bil-i-ty
re-view
ri-dic-u-lous
sat-is-fac-to-ry
Sat-ur-day
scis-sors
screen

29
sec-re-tary
sen-si-ble
sep-a-rate
sev-er-al
sher-iff
sin-cere (-ly)
sleigh
sphere
squir-rel
stat-ure

30
straight
stretched
suc-ceed
sum-ma-rize
sure-ly
sur-prise
tem-po-rary
ter-ri-ble
their
there

31
through-out
to-mor-row
tongue
trea-sur-er
un-for-tu-nate (-ly)
uni-ver-si-ty
us-able
usu-al (-ly)
vac-u-um
valu-able

32
ve-hi-cle
vi-o-lence
vol-un-tary
wan-der
which
whose
width
wreck-age
writ-ing
writ-ten

Weekly Spelling Words: Level 8

1

ab-bre-vi-ate
ab-sence
ab-so-lute (-ly)
ac-cel-er-ate
ac-com-plice
ac-cus-tom (ed)
a-chieve (-ment)
ac-tu-al
ad-e-quate
ad-ver-tise (-ment)

2

a-gainst
a-gree-able
aisle
al-co-hol
all right
al-though
a-lu-mi-num
am-a-teur
a-mend-ment
an-a-lyze

3

an-gle
an-ni-ver-sa-ry
an-noy-ance
a-non-y-mous
ant-arc-tic
anx-i-ety
any-where
a-part-ment
a-pol-o-gize
ap-pli-ca-tion

4

ap-point-ment
ap-pre-ci-ate
ap-prox-i-mate
ar-ti-cle
ar-ti-fi-cial
as-sign (-ment)
as-so-ci-a-tion
ath-let-ic
at-tempt
at-tor-ney

5

au-di-ence
au-thor-i-ty
au-tumn
av-e-nue
awk-ward
bal-loon
bal-lot
bar-gain
bar-rel
bat-tery

6

beau-ti-ful
beg-gar
be-hav-ior
be-lief
be-neath
bi-cy-cle
bliz-zard
bough
bound-a-ry
breathe (v.)

7

brief
bril-liant
bruise
bul-le-tin
buoy-ant
bu-reau
busi-ness
caf-e-te-ria
cam-paign
can-celed

8

can-is-ter
ca-noe
ca-pac-i-ty
car-bu-re-tor
ca-reer
car-riage
cash-ier
cas-se-role
ca-tas-tro-phe
cem-e-ter-y

9

cen-sus
cer-tif-i-cate
change-a-ble
choc-o-late
cir-cum-stance
cit-i-zen
civ-i-li-za-tion
clos-et
co-coa
cof-fee

10

colo-nel
co-los-sal
com-mis-sion
com-mit-ted
com-mit-tee
com-mu-ni-cate
com-pet-i-tive (-ly)
com-plex-ion
con-ceive
con-ces-sion

11

con-demn
con-fi-dence
con-grat-u-late
con-science
con-ser-va-tive
con-tin-u-ous
con-ve-nience
co-op-er-ate
cor-re-spond
coun-ter-feit

12

cou-ra-geous
cour-te-ous
cred-i-tor
cried
crit-i-cize
cu-ri-os-i-ty
cyl-in-der
daugh-ter
dealt
de-ci-sion

13

dec-la-ra-tion
def-i-nite (-ly)
de-li-cious
de-pen-dent
de-scrip-tion
de-serve
de-te-ri-o-rate
de-vel-op (-ment)
de-vice
de-vise

14

di-a-phragm
dif-fer-ence
dif-fi-cul-ty
di-plo-ma
dis-agree-able
dis-as-trous
dis-ci-pline
dis-ease
dis-tin-guish
di-vis-i-ble

15

dor-mi-to-ry
doubt
econ-o-my
ef-fi-cien-cy
eighth
e-lab-o-rate
el-lipse
em-ploy-ee
en-gi-neer
en-thu-si-as-tic

16

en-vel-op (v.)
equipped
e-quiv-a-lent
es-pe-cial-ly
ex-ag-ger-ate
ex-cep-tion-al (-ly)
ex-is-tence
ex-pe-ri-ence
ex-tinct
ex-traor-di-nar-y

Weekly Spelling Words: Level 8

17
fa-cil-i-ties
fas-ci-nate
fa-tigue (d)
fau-cet
fer-tile
fierce
fi-nan-cial (-ly)
fo-li-age
for-eign
for-feit

18
frag-ile
fun-da-men-tal
fur-ther-more
gauge
gen-u-ine
ghet-to
gov-ern-ment
grad-u-a-tion
grate-ful
grue-some

19
guar-an-tee
guard-i-an
guid-ance
gym-na-sium
hap-haz-ard
ha-rass
haz-ard-ous
head-ache
height
hem-or-rhage

20
hoarse
hu-mor-ous
hy-drau-lic
hy-giene
hymn
il-leg-i-ble
im-ag-i-na-tive
im-me-di-ate (-ly)
im-pa-tient
in-cred-i-ble

21
in-def-i-nite-ly
in-fe-ri-or
in-flu-en-tial
in-i-tial
in-sur-ance
in-ter-fere
in-ter-pret
in-ter-rupt
is-land
judg-ment

22
juic-y
knowl-edge
knuck-les
lab-o-ra-to-ry
law-yer
league
lei-sure
li-cense
lieu-ten-ant
lik-able

23
li-quid
lit-er-a-ture
lone-li-ness
lov-able
mag-nif-i-cent
ma-jor-i-ty
man-u-fac-ture
may-or
me-di-um
min-i-a-ture

24
mis-cel-la-neous
mis-chie-vous
mis-sile
mo-not-o-nous
mys-te-ri-ous
na-ive
nec-es-sary
ne-go-ti-ate
nick-el
nine-teenth

25
no-tice-able
nui-sance
o-be-di-ence
of-fense
of-fi-cial
op-po-nent
op-por-tu-ni-ty
or-di-nar-i-ly
out-ra-geous
pam-phlet

26
par-a-lyze
pa-ren-the-ses
par-tial
pa-tience
per-pen-dic-u-lar
per-son-nel
per-suade
pla-teau
pneu-mo-nia
pol-i-ti-cian

27
prai-rie
pre-cede
pre-cious
pre-ci-sion
prej-u-dice
pro-ceed
prom-i-nent
pro-nounce
psy-chol-o-gy
ques-tion-naire

28
quo-tient
re-ceipt
re-ceived
rec-i-pe
reign
res-er-voir
re-sis-tance
res-tau-rant
rhyme
rhythm

29
sal-a-ry
sce-ner-y
sched-ule
seize
sim-i-lar
ski-ing
sou-ve-nir
spa-ghet-ti
squeeze
stat-ue

30
stat-ute
study-ing
sub-tle
suf-fi-cient
syl-la-ble
symp-tom
tar-iff
tech-nique
there-fore
thor-ough (-ly)

31
tour-na-ment
trag-e-dy
tru-ly
typ-i-cal
un-con-scious
unique
un-nec-es-sary
va-ri-ety
var-i-ous
vi-cin-i-ty

32
vil-lain
vis-i-ble
vol-ume
vol-un-teer
weigh
weird
wel-fare
wheth-er
whol-ly
wom-en

Additional Spelling Activities

Consider the ideas and activities listed on this page when planning weekly spelling units.

■ Pretest

Select 20-25 words from the master list in the handbook (568-573) to use as a pretest at the beginning of the year. Students who have mastered these words may not need weekly spelling practice. (You may also want to implement a posttest at the end of the year.)

■ High-Frequency Words

Words from one of the many published high-frequency lists (words student writers use again and again) could be incorporated into the weekly spelling lists or perhaps into midweek spelling minilessons. (You might create sentences containing these high-frequency words for brief dictation sessions.)

■ Commonly Mixed Pairs

Refer to the list of commonly mixed pairs in the handbook (574-694) for additional words to incorporate into the weekly spelling lists or into midweek spelling minilessons. (Some of these words already appear in the master spelling list.)

■ Minilessons

Check the minilessons in this guide related to spelling, or create your own. These activities could be used as spelling practice activities.

■ Systematic Practice

As students practice spelling words, they should be encouraged to employ a basic spelling strategy (*examine, pronounce, cover,* and *write*) and repeat this process three or four times to ensure mastery.

■ Regular Writing

Encourage (or require) students to use words from their weekly spelling lists in journal writings, regular writing assignments, and in other writing-related activities.

■ Prefix and Suffix Work

Students could be provided with a limited number of prefixes and suffixes and then asked to create as many new words as possible, adding these affixes to selected words in the weekly spelling lists.

■ Board Work

Display two or three of the most challenging words from the spelling list on the board during a class period. Announce that the words will be erased at the end of the period, and the students will be expected to spell them correctly on a slip of paper before dismissal.

■ Word Searches

Students could be asked to look for words from their weekly spelling lists in the books, periodicals, and newspapers that they read in class and on their own.

■ Specialized Spelling

Students could be asked to list (and spell correctly) words related to special areas of interest like baseball, astronomy, fashions, and so on. (Students may enjoy creating their own specialized dictionaries.)

■ Quarterly Assessment

Select words from the weekly spelling lists for an end-of-the-quarter assessment test. (Words that are misspelled by many of the students should be worked with again during the next quarter.)

> *"When children write early, their experiments with sounds and symbols produce spellings that may not be entirely correct, but research shows that if these children continue to have ample opportunity to write, they gradually increase their spelling power."*
>
> —DONALD GRAVES

Professional Titles for Language Arts Teachers

We highly recommend the following titles on writing, reading, and teaching for middle-school language arts teachers. All titles are Heinemann-Boynton/Cook publications, unless otherwise indicated.

Active Voice: A Writing Program Across the Curriculum

James Moffett

According to many writing experts, this book offers the best sequence of compositions available in print. The forms of writing cataloged in *Write Source 2000* reflect Moffett's approach to writing instruction.

Authors' Insights: Turning Teenagers into Readers & Writers

Donald R. Gallo, editor

The distinguished voices in young adult literature—from Norma Fox Mazer to Robert Cormier—discuss literature and writing, hitting upon many key issues related to current theory and practice.

In the Middle

Nancie Atwell

Ms. Atwell, a former middle-school language arts teacher in Booth Bay, Maine, details her successful middle-school writing and reading workshops. *In the Middle* contains a clear discussion of workshop procedures, practical advice, techniques for conferring with writers and readers, and many examples of student writing.

Living Between the Lines

Lucy McCormick Calkins with Shelley Harwayne

This book invites teachers to bring new life to the reading-writing workshop and challenges them to rethink the teaching of reading and writing. *Living Between the Lines* includes chapters on keeping a writer's notebook, on introducing wonderful literature, and on experimenting with new workshop ideas.

Mind Matters: Teaching for Thinking

Dan Kirby and Carol Kuykendall

Mind Matters discusses a number of important questions about thinking instruction. One fundamental question is at the core of the book: How can teachers help students develop "thoughtful" habits of the mind?

The Reading/Writing Teacher's Companion

Donald H. Graves

This series of short volumes, by the author of *Writer: Teachers and Children at Work*, includes *Investigate Nonfiction, Experiment with Fiction, Discover Your Own Literacy, Build a Literate Classroom*, and *Explore Poetry*.

Seeking Diversity

Linda Rief

Ms. Rief, an eighth-grade teacher in Durham, New Hampshire, presents an enlightening and stimulating look at her classroom where "the intellectual and emotional needs of her students are the crux of her curriculum." Students and the teacher alike thrive in Ms. Rief's classroom. This book is must reading for all teachers in the middle grades and beyond.

Side By Side: Essays on Teaching to Learn

Nancie Atwell

Each essay in this book helps teachers become more active participants in writing and learning. *Side by Side* is an excellent companion piece to *In the Middle*.

Writers in Training

Rebecka Caplan

This resource helps teachers establish a program of "showing" writing activities. (Available through Dale Seymour Publications.)

Minilessons

The following pages contain more than 70 minilessons that you and your students can use with the *Write Source 2000* handbook. These minilessons cover all the important topics addressed in the handbook.

Minilessons

Minilessons can transform any classroom into an active learning environment. (We define a minilesson as anything that lasts about 10 minutes and covers a single idea or a basic core of knowledge.) Minilessons can be delivered from the front of the room and include the entire class. They can also be individualized or worked into cooperative learning groups. Ideally, each lesson will address a particular need—a need some students are experiencing right now. This makes learning much more meaningful and successful.

Minilessons work very well in the writing workshop classroom. Those people who are "stuck" can be pulled together for 10 minutes each day until they solve their problem. Perhaps one group of students has a need to know how to punctuate dialogue because they are writing stories. Another group of students may need information and practice combining sentences. And still another group may need help with forming possessives. All this (and more) can be scheduled within one class period. The diverse needs of students can be met by teaching them the skills they need . . . when they need to learn them.

The first several pages of the minilessons that follow focus on "The Yellow Pages" section in *Write Source 2000*. They address aspects of punctuation, spelling, usage, grammar, and sentence structure. The remaining pages cover a variety of topics from throughout the handbook. (The suggested level for each minilesson is in parentheses.)

Stop it! . . . . *Using Periods* (6)

- Study the rules in "The Yellow Pages" for using periods (**460-463**).
  WRITE a sentence about something that came to a dead stop—a train, a game, a popcorn popper, or whatever.
  In your sentence, **SHOW** all four uses of the period: after an initial, as a decimal point, at the end of a sentence, and after an abbreviation. (Be inventive!)

Broken Reply . . . . *Using Ellipses* (7)

- Study the guidelines for using ellipses (**465-467**).
  REMEMBER (or imagine) a time when you broke something valuable that belonged to someone else.
  SUPPOSE the owner asks, in pain or in anger, "How did *this* happen?"
  WRITE a broken reply, using ellipses correctly.

Cold Serial . . . . *Commas in a Series* (8)

- Study the guidelines for using commas to separate items in a series (**469**).
  SUPPOSE you won a free, round-trip plane ticket to Antarctica but you may pack only one small suitcase.
  WRITE a complete sentence that lists everything you pack for your f-r-r-r-reezing journey.
  USE commas correctly to separate items in the series.

Sandy Claws .... *Punctuating Clauses and Phrases* (6)

■ Study the guidelines for using commas to separate clauses and phrases from the rest of the sentence (**477, 478, 480 & 481, 482**).

SUPPOSE you brought a rambunctious dog to the beach and it created a major ruckus—ran away with swimsuits, kicked sand into coolers, etc.

WRITE a paragraph about what happened at the beach **MAKE** each sentence demonstrate a different point about the use of commas to separate clauses and phrases.

WRITE another paragraph explaining what each one of your sentences demonstrates.

Keeku! Keeku! .... *Using Semicolons* (7)

■ Study the guidelines for using semicolons (**484-487**).

READ "Fashionation" (**141**).

FIND two sentences that use semicolons; **REWRITE** the independent clauses in them as separate sentences.

FIND two other pairs of sentences that could be joined with a semicolon; **JOIN** them, punctuating correctly.

Lower the flow. .... *Using Colons* (8)

■ Study the guidelines for using colons to introduce a list (**493**). Pay special attention to the samples.

THINK UP three new ways either to control styrofoam waste or to conserve water.

WRITE an *incorrectly punctuated* sentence containing a list of your three items.

TRADE papers with a partner.

WRITE a correct version of your partner's sentence using a colon properly to introduce the items in a series.

Hyphen a Good Time .... *Using Commas and Hyphens* (8)

■ Quickly review the guidelines for both commas (**468-482**) and hyphens (**498-505**).

PUNCTUATE the following sentence correctly so it makes sense:

Two thirds of those fat bellied gap toothed chew spittin' practically brain fried motorcycle maniacs had five mile long prison records.

So to Speak .... *Using Quotation Marks* (7)

■ Study guideline **516** for using quotation marks.
THINK of a distinctive slang word that one of your friends always uses.
WRITE a sentence about your friend, using the word in a special way.
USE quotation marks properly to draw attention to the special use.

Pssst! .... *Using Quotation Marks* (7)

■ Study the guidelines for using double and single quotation marks (**511-515**).
REMEMBER something you said earlier today (or earlier this year).
IMAGINE you overhear two people gossiping about you. (Where are they? How do they know you? What is their attitude toward you?) One is telling the other what you said, using your exact words.
WRITE down their conversation exactly, using double and single quotation marks correctly.

Enchanted, I'm sure. .... *Using Parentheses* (8)

■ You know how sometimes you say one thing and *think* another?
STUDY the guidelines for using parentheses (**532**).
THINK of a time when you met somebody new and said all the polite things.
WRITE a paragraph showing what you said, but in parentheses write down what you *really* thought.

Shopping with the Biggies .... *Capitalization* (6)

■ Study the rules for capitalization (**533-546**).
LIST three or four quite different famous people.
For each famous person, **SUPPOSE** that he or she went shopping for food, brand name clothes, etc.
WRITE each person's shopping list *without* any capital letters.
TRADE papers with a partner and capitalize correctly.
CHECK your partner's work.

Double Vision .... *Forming Plural Nouns* (7)

■ Study the guidelines for forming plural nouns (**547-554**).
SUPPOSE you were attending a national convention of twins; you and your twin are talking with another pair of twins about what a pain it is to have to buy two of everything.
WRITE your conversation in the form of a play script (see **260** for a model), using as many different kinds of plurals as you can.

Digital Readout .... *Writing Numbers* (6)

■ Study the rules for writing numbers correctly (**558-562**).
REWRITE the following sentence correctly:
8 or nine of the twenty-6 seniors, or about 2 point six percent of the entire high school population, had pledged to read 200 200-page books by July Four, Two Thousand A.D.
TRADE papers with a partner and critique your revisions.

E Before I .... *Spelling* (6)

■ Study the exceptions to the "i before e" rule in **564.**
COMPOSE your own sentence containing all of these exceptions: *their, height, counterfeit, foreign*, and *heir*. (Good luck!)

Bad Spellers' Dictionary .... *Spelling* (8)

■ Note "The Yellow Pages Guide to Improved Spelling" (**568-573**).
COMPILE a *Bad Spellers' Dictionary*.
First, **COLLECT** all the words you usually misspell.
Second, **LIST** the words the way you usually spell them (the wrong way).
Finally, after each wrong spelling, **SHOW** the correct spelling.
GIVE your *Bad Spellers' Dictionary* to some poor, needy soul—or keep it for yourself and keep adding to it.

Double Trouble .... *Using the Right Word* (8)

■ Study "The Yellow Pages Guide to Using the Right Word" (**574-694**) until you find a number of pairs of words that you usually mix up.
COPY the model "cumulative" sentence in **113** and study how it's made.
WRITE a sentence with a similar structure but on a topic you choose.
In your sentence, **USE** at least two words wrongly (for example, use "principle" for "principal" and "you're" for "your").
SWITCH papers with a friend. **CHALLENGE** your friend to find and correct the wrongly used words in your sentence.

Door Jam .... *Spotting Subjects and Predicates* (7)

■ Study the sections on subjects and predicates (**696-705**).
READ the story in section **401** about the girl who lost her fingernail.
LIST on a separate sheet the simple subject and simple predicate in each sentence.
PUT a star next to the five most effective subjects and predicates.

Seeing Spots .... *Independent and Dependent Clauses* (6)

■ Study the guidelines for independent and dependent clauses (**710**). Study the Braille alphabet in **799.**

WRITE a complex sentence (a sentence with one independent clause and at least one dependent clause) in *Braille*.

Special Challenge: Translate your sentence into Morse code (**800**) or cuneiform (**801**).

That's Simple .... *Types of Sentences* (8)

■ Study the different types of sentences in **711-714.**

The **WRITE** four sentences about school life. Each sentence should be a different type (simple, compound, complex, and compound-complex).

EXCHANGE your work. Make sure your partner has used the four different types of sentences.

ADD a compound or complex sentence to your partner's writing before you return it.

The Four Stooges on Venus .... *Kinds of Sentences* (7)

■ Study the four different kinds of sentences described in **715-718.**

CREATE four characters—four "stooges"—one who speaks only in *declarative* sentences, another only in *interrogatives*, another only in *imperatives*, another only in *exclamations*.

WRITE a short, funny radio drama about the "Four Stooges" as they step out of their Venusian Landing Vehicle (VLV) onto a weird new planet. (Keep each of the stooges in character.)

HINT: You'll have more to work with if you first study what scientists already know about the atmosphere on Venus.

Pandora's Box .... *Forming Possessives* (6)

■ Review the instructions for forming possessive nouns (**731**) and possessive pronouns (**741**) and for using apostrophes to punctuate singular and plural possessive nouns (**522-523**).

IMAGINE that three teenage brothers and sisters (you may decide the combination) stumble across a box full of their childhood toys. They disagree violently about what toy belongs to whom.

WRITE out their excited (maybe angry, maybe funny) conversation—use play-script format (see **260**) if you wish.

PUT all possessive nouns and pronouns—correctly punctuated, of course—in **ALL CAPS**.

Lost and Found (I) .... *Identifying Types of Nouns* (7)

■ Study the definitions and examples of types of nouns in **719-724.**
On a sheet of paper, **MAKE** three headings: "Concrete Nouns," "Abstract Nouns," and "Collective Nouns."
READ the fascinating biography of Francis Ann Slocum in section **157.**
LIST all the concrete nouns in the biography under the proper heading; do the same for abstract and collective nouns.
PLACE a "c" in parentheses after the word if it is a common noun and a "p" if it is a proper noun.

Lost and Found (II) .... *Identifying Pronouns and Antecedents* (7)

■ Review personal pronouns and antecedents in **733-735.**
READ once again the story of Francis Slocum's life among the Miami Indians (**157**).
LIST all the personal pronouns you can find.
After each pronoun, add a dash and write the antecedent (if you can find one).

And on Your Left .... *Kinds of Pronouns* (7)

■ Review the "Other Types of Pronouns" (besides personal pronouns) in **743-748;** notice the helpful chart after **748.**
Now **SUPPOSE** you landed a job as a tour guide who has to show international visitors all the fascinating sights in your own bedroom. It's your first day of work and you need to practice.
WRITE down a first draft of your spiel.
USE at least one of each kind of pronoun—relative, demonstrative, interrogative, intensive, reflexive, and indefinite.
TRADE papers with someone and challenge him or her to find an example of each different kind of pronoun.

I get a kick out of this. .... *Active and Passive Verbs* (6)

■ Review the definitions of active and passive voice in verbs (**753-754**).
CHOOSE a sport that involves hitting or kicking a ball.
WRITE a paragraph describing a moment of intense action in that sport from the point of view of one of the players; **USE** active verbs.
REWRITE the paragraph, describing the same action from the point of view of the ball; **USE** passive verbs.

Munchies .... *Verb Tenses* (8)

■ Review the sections on verb tenses (**755-760**)—present, past, future, present perfect, past perfect, and future perfect.

THINK about the food you eat.
WRITE sentences about three days' worth of meals and snacks.
START your sentences with the following phrases and **USE** the appropriate verb tense:
By yesterday noon,
Yesterday,
Since yesterday,
Today,
Tomorrow,
Already by noon tomorrow,

All the Right Parts .... *Principal Parts of Irregular Verbs* (8)

■ Study the chart of "Common Irregular Verbs and Their Principal Parts" until you know all the verb forms.

MAKE your own set of flash cards.
PUT the present tense form of a verb on one side; **PUT** the past tense and past participle on the other side.
TRY to stump your neighbor; **ASK** your neighbor to make up sentences using the three principal parts correctly.

Weird Objects: ....*Transitive Verbs; Direct and Indirect Objects* (8)

■ Study the sections on "Transitive Verbs" (**762**), "Direct Object" (**763**), and "Indirect Object" (**764**).

MAKE UP ten weird sentences using your own combinations from the following lists:

VERBS	INDIRECT OBJECTS	DIRECT OBJECTS
force-fed	ostrich	sandwich
tossed	catcher's mitt	medicine ball
handed	piano tuner	love letter
left	carburetor	BB
floated	jellyfish	jungle gym

"To Be" or Not "To Be" .... *Intransitive Verbs* (8)

■ **FIND** and **JOT DOWN** at least two intransitive verbs in the one-paragraph book review of *Tom Sawyer* (**190**).

For another challenge, **FIND** and **JOT DOWN** two intransitive verbs in another writng model in the handbook.

Caution: Don't call a verb intransitive if it is in the passive voice (**754, 762**) or if it has a gerund (**768**) or an infinitive (**770**) or a noun phrase (**709**) for an object.

Beyond Awesome, Different, and Cool .... *Degrees of Adjectives and Adverbs* (7)

■ Study the positive, comparative, and superlative forms of adjectives (**779-784**) and adverbs (**787**).

THINK of three different things to compare—three roller coasters, three movies, three flavors of pizza, etc.—where one seems good, another better, and the third best (or bad, worse, and worst).

SUPPOSE one friend describes the three things as "awesome, more awesome, and most awesome"; another retorts, "No man, they are cool, cooler, and coolest!"

Not satisfied, you **WRITE** your own critique of the three.

USE the three degrees of adjectives and adverbs effectively in your critique.

Club Ed .... *Journal Writing* (7)

■ Wonder how to get started writing in a journal? Why not look over the advice on starting a journal in section **131-132**? Check out the idea of writing in a learning log (more on that in **409**). Then,

READ the opening pages of *Write Source 2000*, "An Invitation to Learning" (**001-002**). Focus on what the writer means by "Club Ed."

WRITE in your journal whatever thoughts come to your mind about learning that you experience outside the classroom. Don't settle for the first thoughts that pop up. Keep digging. How many kinds of things do you learn "on the outside"? How is learning outside of school different from learning in school? What would learning be like inside school, if you had *your* way?

Sprints and Marathons .... *Managing Your Time* (6)

■ Under the heading "Managing Your Time" (**452**), pay special attention to the point labeled "Turn big jobs into smaller jobs."

THINK of a job you must do (now or later) that will take more than one day to accomplish.

BREAK that job down into smaller jobs that will each take no more than one hour.

LIST all the smaller jobs under the heading of the one big task. **GROUP** them under subheadings if that will help.

Everybody, shut up! .... *Improving Group Skills* (8)

■ Suppose you are the secretary for your school's student council—maybe you really are! Suppose your group, like many groups, is having a hard time getting anything accomplished because everybody talks and nobody listens.

STUDY carefully the guidelines for "Group Skills" in sections **432-449.**

Quickly **REVIEW** the guidelines for writing summaries (**184-186**).

WRITE a solid summary of "Group Skills" to submit to your student council as a recommendation.

It was a dark and stormy night. .... *Writing Openings* (7)

■ Think of a story from your life that you've been saving to tell somebody.

READ section **019,** "Writing an Opening or Lead Paragraph."

WRITE your most interesting opening paragraph for your story.

GIVE your opening paragraph to someone else to read.

ASK that person to write down whatever questions the opening makes them want answered.

REWRITE the opening so that it raises even better questions.

GIVE your opening to your reader again and repeat the process.

Off the Beaten Path .... *Offbeat Questions* (7)

■ Get a feel for the "Offbeat" or "Unstructured" questions in **038**.

Then **WRITE** an "offbeat" question (and an offbeat answer) about a certain place, object, or event.

WRITE two more offbeat questions and answers about your subject; **SHARE** your work with a classmate.

Twenty-Five Steps .... *"Found" Writing Ideas* (7)

■ Look over section **033,** "Creating a Writing 'SourceBank'," and pay special attention to the subsection " 'Found' Writing Ideas."

JUMP in the air and **SPIN** (with your teacher's permission). Don't move your feet when you land.

TAKE 25 steps in the direction your feet are pointing—of course, you should stop if you come to a wall or any other immovable object.

WRITE fast and furiously about whatever you see from there or whatever comes to your mind.

Fanning Out .... *Clustering* (6)

■ Choose one of the topics from the "Essentials of Life Checklist" in **036.**

USE that word as the "nucleus word" for a cluster that you create.

FOLLOW the directions for clustering in **035.**

At the end of your clustering, **CHOOSE** the one word you've written that would make the most interesting topic for writing.

WRITE FREELY about your topic for 5-10 minutes in class or on your own time.

Whose Pants These Are .... *Imitating a Poem* (8)

■ Read and appreciate the poem "Stopping by Woods on a Snowy Evening" by Robert Frost (**229**). Pay attention to the line length, the rhyme scheme, the rhythm, the subject, the word choice, the mood, etc.

WRITE a "parody" (a playfully twisted imitation) of Frost's poem. First,

CHANGE the word "woods" in the first line to any other word that makes some kind of sense (pants, gloves, car, house, cheese, pen, etc.).

ALTER the rest of the first line so that it fits your new word but still sounds "sort of" like Frost.

FINISH the poem in the same way. Don't be afraid to let your new poem take off on its own if it "wants" to.

Goal to Go .... *Goal Setting* (7)

■ In the section on "Individual Skills" (**450-457**), read with special care about "Setting Goals" (**450-451**). On paper,

WRITE DOWN one goal for next hour.

WRITE DOWN one goal for tonight.

WRITE DOWN one goal for tomorrow.

WRITE DOWN one goal for next week.

WRITE DOWN one goal for next year.

WRITE DOWN one goal for your life.

Alphabet Cluster .... *Selecting a Writing Subject* (8)

■ Read the directions for "Clustering" under "Selecting a Writing Subject" (**035**).
ASK your nearest neighbor to pick any letter of the alphabet.
WRITE DOWN a word that comes to mind starting with that letter.
USE that word as the "nucleus word" for a cluster.
DEVELOP your cluster until you run out of ideas.
PICK an idea from your cluster and **WRITE** about it for 8 minutes.

Byte Into This .... *Computers and Writing* (8)

■ Remind yourself of the steps involved in personal research and in writing a "research story" (**265-270**). Then read the short section on "Computers and Writing" (**287**). If you know how to use a computer, then do this personal research project:
THINK of two people you know about equally well. You must be interested enough in them to write character sketches about them (see **159-165**).
WRITE one character sketch in pencil or pen.
WRITE the second character sketch on a computer. Afterward,
RATE the two sketches on (1) time each took to write, (2) amount of prewriting, (3) length, (4) amount of drafting and revising, and (5) quality of writing.
WRITE UP your experience in a personal research report.

Butcher, Baker, Candlestick Maker .... *Ideas for Short Stories* (8)

■ Read the hilarious and insightful interview with the story writer Bob Kann (**239**). Then look over the "Essentials of Life Checklist" (**036**).
CHOOSE one "essential of life" from each of the three columns.
MAKE UP three characters, each one associated with one of your three "essentials of life."
BEGIN to write a story in which all three characters are forced to interact. **WRITE** the story to *find out* what they do.
WRITE fast and furiously for 5-8 minutes. Then **MAKE NOTES** to help you finish the story later.

Dear Mr. Zzyzz: .... *Writing a Business Letter* (8)

■ Study the instructions for writing a business letter (**203-214**). Memorize the format called "Semiblock" (**204**). Next,
GO THROUGH the list of "Writing Topics" in section **040** and pick any topic that especially interests you. Next,
PICK any name at random from your city's telephone book. Next,
WRITE a business letter in semiblock form asking the person you've picked if he or she has any special information about your topic.

Between Covers .... *Parts of a Book* (7)

■ Review the description of "Parts of a Book" in section **301**.
STUDY the parts and organization of *Write Source 2000.*
PUT a check mark in section **301** by each part that *Write Source 2000* contains.
LIST other parts of *Write Source 2000* that are not mentioned in **301**.

Why We Hiccup .... *Exercises in Style* (6)

■ Under "Writing Topics" (**040**), notice the prompts under the subheading "Explaining . . . the causes of . . . ."
CHOOSE one of the topics.
PRETEND you are a kindergartner and write an explanation of the cause of, say, a tornado or a hiccup.
Now **SWITCH**. **PRETEND** you are an 80-year-old man or woman; **EXPLAIN** the causes of the same thing from that point of view.

Sharpened Ax Today .... *Exercises in Style* (8)

■ Browse around in the sections on "Styling Sentences" (**109-111**).
IMAGINE you are somebody quite different from who you are: an astronaut, a Miss America candidate, an ax murderer, a cab driver, a dolphin trainer, etc.
WRITE one page of that person's daily diary in the style you imagine that person would have. **MAKE** the style clearly different from your own.

Through Different Lenses .... *Writing About Experiences* (7)

■ Review the sections on "Writing About Experiences" (**144-149**).
CHOOSE an experience you've always wanted to tell about.
TURN to the list of "Writing Forms" in section **041.**
CHOOSE one writing form from each of the four categories: personal writing, creative writing, subject writing, and persuasive writing.
WRITE four versions of your experience, one in each different form.

My Partner, 'Tis of Thee .... *Writing Biography* (6)

■ Brush up on techniques of interviewing (see section **405-407**).
STUDY the directions for writing a "Bio-Poem" (**158**).
CHOOSE a partner from the class.
INTERVIEW your partner until you have found out enough information to complete a "bio-poem."
WRITE a bio-poem about your partner and give it to him or her as a gift.

Eyes Like Meteors .... *Writing a Character Sketch* (8)

■ Read through the sections on writing a "Character Sketch" (**159-165**).
CHOOSE the person whom you either love most or admire most in your life.
REMIND yourself of the important ideas about detailed, colorful language in sections **118-122.**
MAKE two headings: "Physical Characteristics" and "Personal Characteristics."
Under each heading, **LIST** the finest details you can observe or remember.
CONCLUDE by writing a sentence that tells your single, strongest impression of that person. Don't settle for vague language here.

Genius Born to Humble Parents .... *Writing the News Story* (6)

■ Read the chapter in *Write Source 2000* on "Writing the News Story" (**171-176**).
WRITE a brief but complete news article, with headline, which reports your own birth as a newsworthy event.
RESEARCH your news article by interviewing your parents.

Credit Where Credit Is Due .... *Citing Borrowed Works* (8)

■ Consult the "Model Works Cited Entries" chart in section **283.**
DECIDE what kind of work *Write Source 2000* is.
WRITE a correct bibliographic entry citing *Write Source 2000.*

This egg has crud on it. .... *Letter of Complaint* (7)

■ Read the guidelines for writing a letter of complaint (**214**).
THINK of a product you've bought that doesn't work well enough or a service you've received that was not performed well enough.
FIND out the address of the person who should receive your complaints.
WRITE a letter of complaint to that person.
PUT your letter in "Full-Block" format as described in section **204.**

Journey to the Center of the Problem .... *Personal Research* (7)

■ Read and enjoy the *Write Source 2000* tips on doing "Personal Research" (**265-270**). Pay special attention to the four points under "Connecting: Telling Your Research Story" (**270**).
REMEMBER a time in your life when you discovered something for yourself by tracking down the answer, maybe by talking to other people.
JOT DOWN whatever you remember that fits under the four headings: (1) What I Knew, (2) What I Wanted to Know, (3) What I Found Out, and (4) What I Learned.
WRITE a "research story" based on your notes.

Food from the Table .... *Using Tables* (6)

■ Study the pages titled "Planet Profusion" in the Student Almanac (**809**). Pay special attention to the table of facts about the planets.

PICK OUT three different planets from the table.
STUDY the facts about each one—gravity, length of year, temperature, etc.
PRETEND you are on the planets, equipped for survival.
WRITE an imaginative observation report telling what your experience is like on each of the three different planets.

My Room, No, My Bottom Drawer! .... *Prewriting: Listing* (6)

■ Survey the "Personal Writing Sampler" (**149**) and choose one type of memory to write about.

NOTICE the instructions for "Listing" under "Selecting a Writing Subject" (**036**).
LIST as many thoughts and details as you can in connection with the memory you chose.
READ your list and pull together several of the most interesting items on it.
WRITE DOWN a *new* and *sharper* focus for your personal writing.

"Out at the Plate" .... *Titles* (7)

■ Read the comments on choosing titles in section **025.**

THINK of your entire life so far.
ASSUME that you've already written a fascinating autobiography (the story of your life). (See **133-143**.)
WRITE *five* of the best titles you can think of for your autobiography.
CHOOSE the best one and **WRITE** it in big letters someplace where you'll see it often.

Once Upon a Coffin .... *Short Story Sampler* (6)

■ Survey the section on "Story Writing" (**237-252**), especially the section on "A Short Story Sampler" (**247-252**).

FORM a circle with your class or a large group. (This can be fun at a party!)
SET OUT to write a horror story.
WRITE the first sentence of your story on a piece of paper as everyone else does the same.
PASS your paper to the person next to you.
WRITE a second sentence on the sheet your neighbor passes to you. *Remember:* You're trying to write a horror story. Try to catch the spirit of your partner's story and keep it up.
CONTINUE adding sentences and passing papers until your own sheet goes all around the circle and comes back to you.
DO THE SAME for a mystery, a fantasy, a science-fiction story, a myth, or a fable.

Road Trip .... *Writing Dialogue* (6)

■ Read the "Guidelines for Developing Dialogue" (**255-256**).
INVENT two characters: one male, one female, one older, and one younger.
GIVE each character at least a couple of conflicting character traits (she's smart but impatient, or he's brave but depressed). Make a note of the character traits.
PUT the two characters in a car and have them talking.
WRITE three different snatches of conversation. In the first, make them *contented*.. In the second, make them *upset*. In the third, make them *afraid*. (Make sure each one's distinctive character traits show through in their conversation.)

Capriccio/Mangel-wurzel/Zapateado .... *Using the Dictionary* (6)

■ Thoroughly study the section on "Using the Dictionary" (**303-304**).
CHOOSE an unusual word that starts with the first two letters of your last name. Try to find a word that has a full and fairly lengthy entry in the dictionary.
READ every word and abbreviation in the dictionary entry.
WRITE an essay in which you express in full sentences and with logical organization every single piece of information you can gather from the dictionary entry.

Question Maker .... *Selecting a Writing Topic* (8)

■ Look at the "Essentials of Life Checklist" (**036**).
CREATE five different topics by picking one word from each of the three columns and making a good question out of it: for example,

CLOTHING MACHINES RULES/LAWS
"What laws apply to the machines that manufacture clothing?"
SENSES PLANTS FUEL
"What does a log sound like when it burns?"

If any of the questions lead you to a better idea, **WRITE** about it.

Mind if I tape this? .... *Interviewing/Creative Collaboration* (7)

■ Study the sections on "Interviewing" (**405-407**).
ASK your friend to **PRETEND** to be someone he or she always dreamed of being. Your friend should try to imagine as much as possible about what that person's life is like.
PUT ON your best interviewing behavior and interview your friend.
WRITE out the best questions you can think of—the kind the interviewee is best prepared to answer.
BE PREPARED to go beyond your questions as the interview develops.

Polysyllables . . . . *Improving Vocabulary* (8)

■ Survey the section on "Improving Vocabulary" (**371-384**); know how to use the lists of prefixes (**374-375**), suffixes (**377**), and roots (**378-384**).

USE the three lists to figure out the definitions of the following words:

philanthropy
prestidigitation
pneumoconiosis
antidisestablishmentarianism

CHECK your definitions against an unabridged dictionary.

"Can't See the Monkeys from the Bus" . . . . *Creative Thinking* (6)

■ Consult the list of "Writing Topics" (**040**) under the subheading "Describing . . . People . . . Places . . . Things." You might want to

READ the sections under the heading "Thinking Creatively" (**331-342**). Also

READ the short sections on "Writing Your Own Poem" (**224-228**).

From the list of people, places, and things, **PICK** one person, one place, and one thing. (*Hint:* Pick a *weird* combination.)

WRITE a poem in which the *person* you chose talks about the *thing* in the *place*. (For example, a bus driver talks about a billboard at the zoo.)

Dear Sis, ... *Improving Reading* (8)

■ Suppose your school has assigned you to be a Big Brother or Big Sister of a younger student who is having trouble reading and remembering.

STUDY the chapter on "Study-Reading Skills" (**361-370**).

MAKE UP a name for your student.

WRITE a personal letter (see **196-202**) in which you give your student the best advice you know of for improving his or her reading.

Playing Teach . . . . *Understanding Essay Tests* (8)

■ Carefully study the advice on taking essay tests in section **421-427.**

GATHER together some knowledge that you recently gained in one of your non-English classes.

WRITE a good-quality essay-test question to give to a student who takes that course next year.

SUBMIT your test question to the teacher of that course for a critique.

Unless what? . . . . *Finding a Subject* (6)

■ Read the paragraph on "Free Writing" under "Selecting a Writing Subject" (**035**).

WRITE the word "Unless" on a piece of paper and finish writing the sentence any way you can.

CONTINUE writing, going wherever your fertile mind takes you.

After 5-8 minutes, **STOP** and **WRITE** the single most important thought that has occurred to you during that time, whether you've written it yet or not.

All systems are go. . . . . *Taking Inventory of Your Thoughts* (7)

■ Choose a starting point for a new piece of writing using the ideas in section **034.** Especially notice the suggestions under "Personal Almanac (Inventory)" and "Life Map." Try to decide on a topic in 2-3 minutes.

USE topic number **016**, "Taking Inventory of Your Thoughts," to collect and focus your ideas.

Quickly **WRITE** down everything you can think of about

(1) your present **situation** as a writer,
(2) your **self** (what would this writing mean for you?),
(3) your **subject**,
(4) your **readers**, and
(5) your **style** of writing (form, approach, manner, language, etc.).

CHANGE one of these five—for example, *narrow* your subject, or aim at a *different kind of reader*.

DECIDE and **WRITE DOWN** how the other four factors will be forced to change in view of your first change.

Have *I* Got Problems. . . . . *Word Problems* (6)

■ Study the "Guidelines for Solving Word Problems." Look for "Word problems" in the index.

THINK of a situation in your own life that involves measures, distances, times, costs, weights, rates, or fractions.

WRITE up your situation in the form of a word problem (also known as a story problem). **GIVE** your word problem to a neighbor in class to solve.

Croak/Cash In/Kick the Bucket .... *Using the Thesaurus* (7)

■ Read the instructions for "Using the Thesaurus" in section **302.**
CHOOSE one of the following pairs of words: *find / lose, sober / drunk, build / destroy.*
LOOK UP both words in a thesaurus.
WRITE a paragraph explaining the difference you notice between the language we use for something good and for something bad.

One hand washes the other. .... *Symbols of Correction* (8)

■ See the "Symbols of Correction" on the last page of *Write Source 2000.*
EXCHANGE papers with a partner—use any paper you've written earlier and still care about.
EDIT your partner's paper, using the correction symbols wherever possible.
ADD a written comment that conveys your *personal* response to your partner's paper as a whole.

Hitting the Stacks .... *Using the Reference Section* (6)

■ Read through the section listing reference books of special interest to young people (**298**).
SELECT a book from the list that you haven't heard of before.
GO to the library and find out how to use the book—what to look for in it, how to save time using it, etc.
WRITE a note summarizing your discoveries about the book.
GIVE the note to a neighbor in your class.

The *Write Source 2000* Language Program

Overview

How does the program work?

There are four main components in the program: **(1)** the **Write Source 2000** student handbook; **(2)** the **Write Source 2000 Teacher's Guide; (3)** the **SourceBook** of activities for each grade level, 6-8, plus the **Teacher's Edition** for each SourceBook; and **(4)** the **Daily Language Workouts** for each grade level, 6-8. Here's how the different components can work in your classroom:

1 The **Write Source 2000** handbook can be used alone as a schoolwide resource for writing thinking, and learning. (The handbook serves as the students' core resource for all three years.)

2 With the addition of the **Teacher's Guide,** teachers have basic planning ideas, start-up activities, and minilessons to use when developing a writing and learning program.

3 The **SourceBook** at each grade level, 6-8, provides teachers with a comprehensive collection of writing and learning activities. Teachers can customize their own writing-based language curriculum by selecting those activities appropriate for their students. (The **Teacher's Edition** for each grade level provides timetables, teacher's notes, as well as the appropriate SourceBook answer key.)

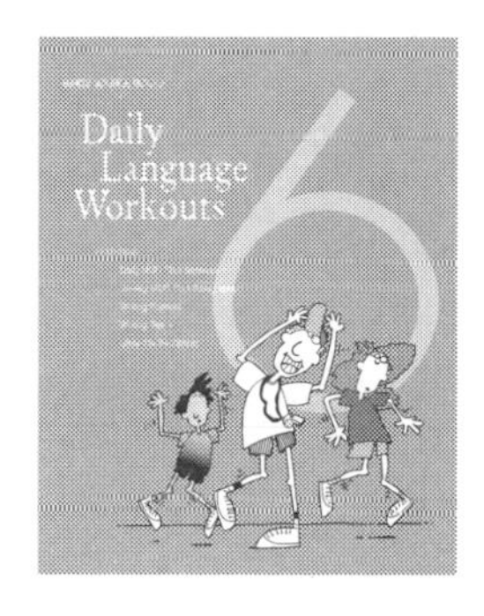

4 The **Daily Language Workouts,** grades 6-8, offer proofreading sentences and paragraphs, writing prompts, writing topics, and show-me sentences.

What are the SourceBooks?

The student SourceBooks provide teachers with a rich resource of more than 180 writing, language, and learning activities to choose from when planning a language program. (There is a separate SourceBook for each grade: 6, 7, and 8.)

It's important for teachers to understand that this is an instructional resource book, not a student workbook, and that the activities should be used selectively depending on the needs and nature of the students.

What types of activities do the SourceBooks contain?

The activities break down in the following way:

- 7 Core Writing Units
- 10 Prewriting Strategies
- 10 Forms of Writing
- 7 Revising Workshops
- 6 Sentence-Combining Workshops
- 10 Editing Workshops
- 8 Proofreading Workshops
- 15 Language Workshops
- 9 Reading and Learning Strategies
- 8 Talking and Listening Activities
- 9 Vocabulary and Word Play Activities
- 50 Writing and Learning Minilessons
- 15 Thinking Workshops

(These numbers may vary slightly from level to level.)

How are the SourceBook activities sequenced?

In some cases, the activities within certain sections of the SourceBook build upon one another—provide a sequence, if you will. In many other cases, the activities can be implemented as the teacher chooses. Teachers should also know that certain skills and strategies covered at one level may be addressed again at another level for reinforcement. And in some cases, activities build on one another from level to level. (Suggested year-long timetables are provided in each grade-level SourceBook Teacher's Edition.)

What types of writing are included in the SourceBooks?

This chart lists many of the types of writing found in the SourceBooks. The boldfaced activities are Core Writing Units. (See page 25 in this guide for a framework of the handbook writing activities.)

	6	7	8
PERSONAL WRITING			
Recording	Collecting Ideas (67-78) Writing for Fluency (85)	Collecting Ideas (69-80) Journal Writing (237)	Collecting Ideas (65-76) Empathizing (213)
Recalling and Remembering	**Writing About Personal Experiences** (5) Writing a Creative Sketch (81) Writing a Monologue (94)	**Writing About Personal Experiences** (5) Observing and Recording (80) The Autobiography (83)	**Writing the Phase Autobiography** (5) Personal Journal Writing (79) Writing Anecdotes (81)
SUBJECT WRITING			
Introducing	**Writing Descriptively About People** (25) Bio-Poems (91)	**Writing a Character Sketch** (27) Writing About People (84)	**Writing the Phase Biography** (23) Character Sketch (87)
Describing	Selecting Details (103) Showing vs. Telling (104)	Describing a Place (85) Describing an Event (92)	Describing an Object (80) Using Sensory Detail (101)
Reporting	Reporting on Events (87)	Finding the Main Idea (183, 184) The Editorial Cartoon (188)	News Stories (82) Objective Writing (223)
Corresponding	Friendly Letters (83) Writing an Invitation (221)	Letter Writing (87) Creative Questions (210)	Letter of Advice (220) Letter to Editor (224)
Informing	**Building Paragraphs 1: Narrative Writing** (11) **Building Paragraphs 2: Expository & Descriptive** (19)	**Building Paragraphs 1: Supporting Details** (13) **Building Paragraphs 2: Planning Strategies** (21)	**Building Paragraphs: Expository Writing** (11) **Building Essays** (17)
Searching and Researching	**Writing a Report** (55) Know-Want-Learn (185) Investigating Local History (219) Summarizing (248A)	**Writing a Report** (55) Know-Want-Learn (182) Summarizing As You Read (186) Personal Research (240)	Oral History (199) Interviewing (200) Paraphrasing (214)
CREATIVE WRITING			
Translating	Phase Poetry (92) Concrete Poetry (229)	A Thinking Poem (205) Analyzing/Translating (220)	Playing with Poetry (232, 233) Bombastic Proverbs (234)
Inventing	**Writing Mystery Stories** (35) Writing Fables (93)	**Writing Myths** (33) Inventing (214)	**Writing a Survival Story** (33) Building a Story (89)
Scripting	Instant Improv (204) TV Skit (220)	Interviewing (195)	Impromptu Miniplay (203) Story of Speculation (212)
REFLECTIVE WRITING			
Analyzing and Classifying	**Writing the Comparison and Contrast Essay** (47) Analyzing a Process (226) Pro-Con (225)	**Writing About Problems and Solutions** (41) Comparison/Contrast (90) Observing/Analyzing (211)	**Cause and Effect Writing** (41) **Writing to Define** (49) Comparing/Contrasting (221)
Persuading	Brainstorming/Persuading (213) Pretending/Persuading (224)	Speaking Persuasively (196)	Arguing/Judging (225) Compromising (227)
Reviewing	Writing Book Reviews (89)	Writing Book Reviews (88)	Writing a Book Review (85) Compiling a Review (86)

What other kinds of activities are included in the SourceBooks?

Each *SourceBook* contains activities that will help students **start** writing, others that will help them **continue** writing, and still other activities that will help them **complete** their writing.

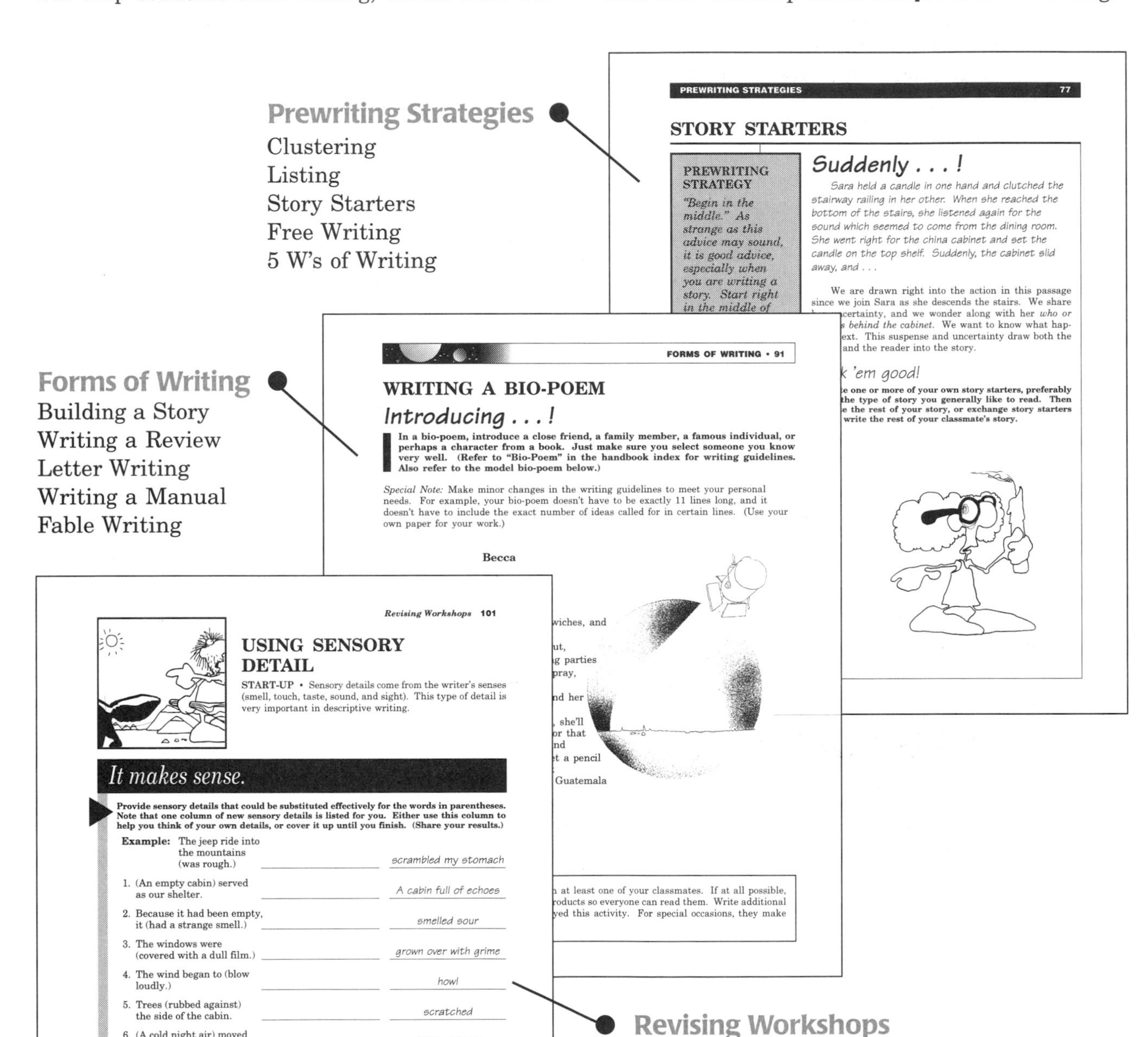

Prewriting Strategies
Clustering
Listing
Story Starters
Free Writing
5 W's of Writing
PREWRITING STRATEGIES 77
STORY STARTERS
PREWRITING STRATEGY
"Begin in the middle." As strange as this advice may sound, it is good advice, especially when you are writing a story. Start right in the middle of
Suddenly . . . !
Sara held a candle in one hand and clutched the stairway railing in her other. When she reached the bottom of the stairs, she listened again for the sound which seemed to come from the dining room. She went right for the china cabinet and set the candle on the top shelf. Suddenly, the cabinet slid away, and . . .
We are drawn right into the action in this passage since we join Sara as she descends the stairs. We share
Forms of Writing
Building a Story
Writing a Review
Letter Writing
Writing a Manual
Fable Writing
FORMS OF WRITING • 91
WRITING A BIO-POEM
Introducing . . . !
In a bio-poem, introduce a close friend, a family member, a famous individual, or perhaps a character from a book. Just make sure you select someone you know very well. (Refer to "Bio-Poem" in the handbook index for writing guidelines. Also refer to the model bio-poem below.)
Special Note: Make minor changes in the writing guidelines to meet your personal needs. For example, your bio-poem doesn't have to be exactly 11 lines long, and it doesn't have to include the exact number of ideas called for in certain lines. (Use your own paper for your work.)
Becca
Revising Workshops 101
USING SENSORY DETAIL
START-UP • Sensory details come from the writer's senses (smell, touch, taste, sound, and sight). This type of detail is very important in descriptive writing.
It makes sense.
Provide sensory details that could be substituted effectively for the words in parentheses. Note that one column of new sensory details is listed for you. Either use this column to help you think of your own details, or cover it up until you finish. (Share your results.)
Example: The jeep ride into the mountains (was rough.) scrambled my stomach
1. (An empty cabin) served as our shelter. A cabin full of echoes
2. Because it had been empty, it (had a strange smell.) smelled sour
3. The windows were (covered with a dull film.) grown over with grime
4. The wind began to (blow loudly.) howl
5. Trees (rubbed against) the side of the cabin. scratched
6. (A cold night air) moved in as the storm left. A frigid front
7. (An amazing quiet) followed the storm. A penetrating calm
8. A spring (softly poured) fresh, cool water. purred
9. (A soft moss) covered the ground. Green velvet
10. The view (was beautiful.) was breathtaking
© Houghton Mifflin Company. All rights reserved.
Revising Workshops
Reviewing First Drafts
Group Advising
Supporting Opinions
Showing Versus Telling

Sentence-Combining Workshops

Combining with Key Words
Combining with Phrases
Combining with Adverb Clauses
Combining with Adjective Clauses

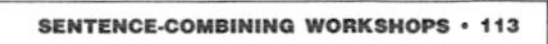

COMBINING SENTENCES WITH PHRASES

Transplanting Phrases

THE FIRST STEP • Ideas from short sentences can be combined into longer units of thought by moving a **phrase** from one sentence to the other. It's almost like **transplant** surgery. To learn how to transplant phrases in your own writing, you'll need the help of your handbook. (Refer to "Phrase, Combining with" in the index.) After you carefully review this information, move on to the workshop that follows.

Combine each pair of simple sentences using the phrase asked for in parentheses. The first four are done for you. Study these examples carefully before you begin work on the rest of the workshop.

1. That spaghetti sauce tastes gross.
   It's cooking on the stove.

cooking on the stove ______ tastes gross.

t the department store ______ yesterday.

ot.

to get an A on the test ______.

ok.
hater.

book hater ______, was actually reading a book.

______, Marion turned into a prune.

EDITING FOR CLARITY

"It's a Superflooz VII Intergalactic Spacezipper!"

1. **Read the paragraph below. It contains a number of words, phrases, and sentences which are unclear and could easily mislead the reader.**
2. **Locate one example of each type of error listed beneath the paragraph; write the number of the sentence in which you found each error on the blank provided. (Refer to your handbook index for help. Each type of error is listed there.)**
3. **Then correct each error in the paragraph itself. (Rewrite those sentences which need major revising on the lines provided.)**

(1) Learning to pilot a Superflooz VII Intergalactic Spacezipper at ultra light speed is really much easier than it sounds. (2) First, the pilot must strap himself into the control seat so he can't ~~hardly~~ move. (3) Then he must switch on the viewing screen. (4) This special screen nearly allows the pilot to see for five miles. (5) At this point, the pilot must switch on the Magno-Zip Atombooster. (6) This switch is located just above the pilot's head and looks sort of like a radish. (7) One of the switches ~~are~~ is green and should not be touched at all, for it will activate the ship's destruct mechanism. (8) After warming up for three minutes, the pilot can throw the switch for the Magno-Zip Atombooster to the no-return position. (9) The pilot must remember ... Atombooster. (10) If he follows all of these ... a smooth trip.

____ Pronoun problem (agreement)
____ Misplaced modifier (phrase)
...eement of subject and verb

... pages in your handbook that begin with "Problems ...ms" in your index). Make note of one "problem" on this activity. Also, note how to correct the problem.

Editing Workshops

Correcting Sentence Errors
Editing for Clarity
Using the Right Word

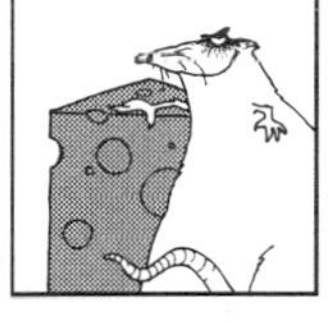

END PUNCTUATION REVIEW

START-UP • Punctuation, along with capitalization, controls the movement of your writing. The end punctuation marks—periods, question marks, exclamation points—signal the end of a sentence. Commas signal the breaks or pauses in a sentence. Considering these two simple points, punctuation—especially end punctuation—is not a difficult part of writing.

Say cheese!

Place periods, question marks, and exclamation points where they are needed in the following narrative. Also supply the necessary capital letters. (Refer to "Punctuation, marking" in your handbook index for rules and examples.)

Example: I had applied for a position on the yearbook staff during the first week of school. What a thrill to find out I made it! Was I going to be able to do a good job? I would find out on group picture day.

my friends and i were very excited that it was finally group picture day carrie, kim, and i were responsible for making sure that everybody who was in a group got his or her picture taken what a difficult job how could we be sure that everybody would be in the right place at the right time were we up to this task we were about to find out

we decided that the teachers themselves should make sure that all of their activity members were at the right place at the right time for the pictures we told the teachers to check off the students' names as they

Proofreading Workshops

Reviewing Capitalization
Using Commas
Punctuating Dialogue
Using Apostrophes
Punctuation Review

Additional SourceBook Activities

The SourceBooks also contain activities to help students become more proficient users of the language. Other activities address reading and learning, talking and listening, thinking, and vocabulary and word play.

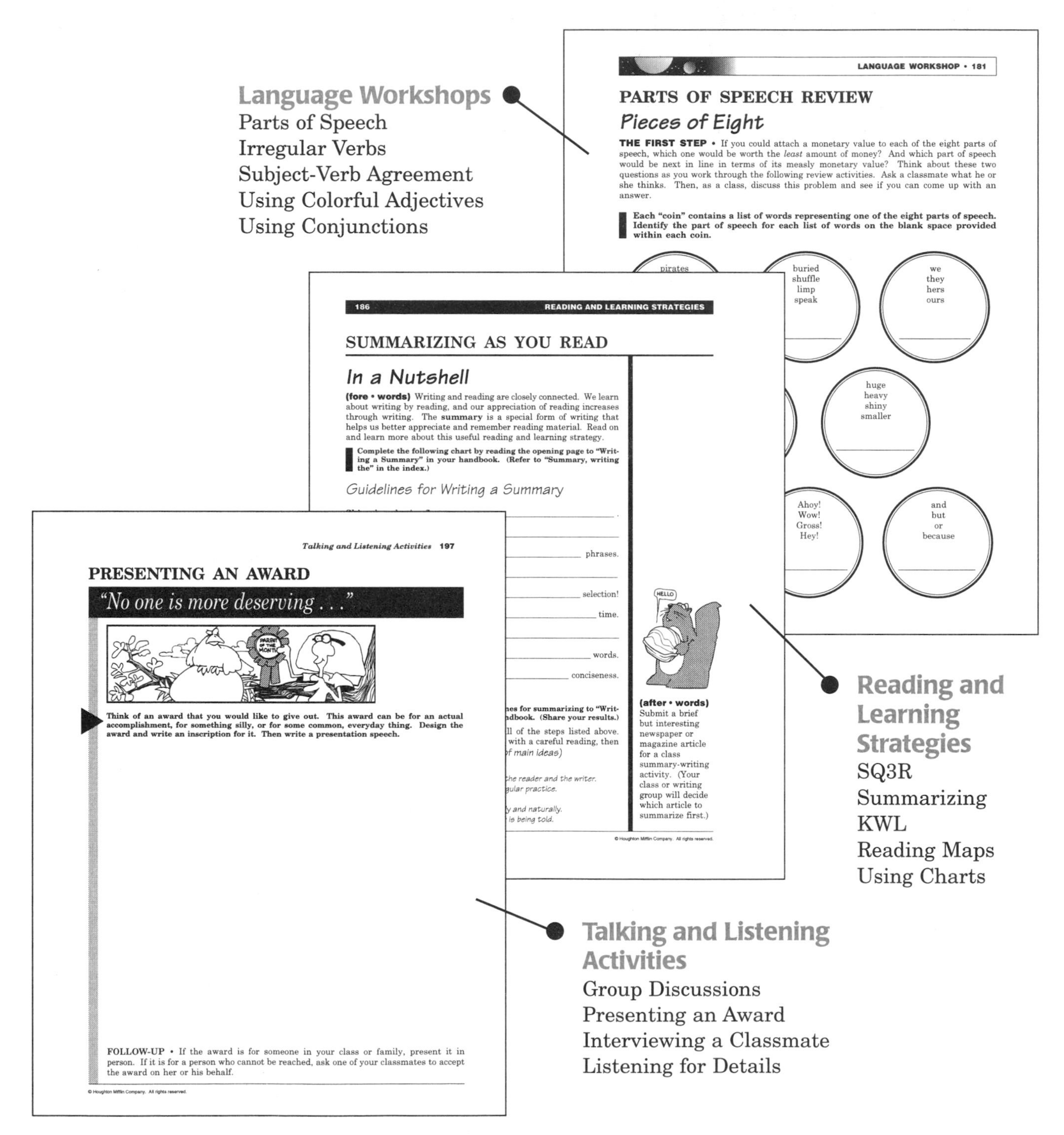

LANGUAGE WORKSHOP • 181
PARTS OF SPEECH REVIEW
Pieces of Eight
THE FIRST STEP • If you could attach a monetary value to each of the eight parts of speech, which one would be worth the least amount of money? And which part of speech would be next in line in terms of its measly monetary value? Think about these two questions as you work through the following review activities. Ask a classmate what he or she thinks. Then, as a class, discuss this problem and see if you can come up with an answer.
Each "coin" contains a list of words representing one of the eight parts of speech. Identify the part of speech for each list of words on the blank space provided within each coin.
buried shuffle limp speak
we they hers ours
huge heavy shiny smaller
Ahoy! Wow! Gross! Hey!
and but or because
186
READING AND LEARNING STRATEGIES
SUMMARIZING AS YOU READ
In a Nutshell
(fore • words) Writing and reading are closely connected. We learn about writing by reading, and our appreciation of reading increases through writing. The summary is a special form of writing that helps us better appreciate and remember reading material. Read on and learn more about this useful reading and learning strategy.
Complete the following chart by reading the opening page to "Writing a Summary" in your handbook. (Refer to "Summary, writing the" in the index.)
Guidelines for Writing a Summary
HELLO
(after • words) Submit a brief but interesting newspaper or magazine article for a class summary-writing activity. (Your class or writing group will decide which article to summarize first.)
© Houghton Mifflin Company. All rights reserved.
Talking and Listening Activities 197
PRESENTING AN AWARD
"No one is more deserving . . ."
PARENT OF THE MONTH
Think of an award that you would like to give out. This award can be for an actual accomplishment, for something silly, or for some common, everyday thing. Design the award and write an inscription for it. Then write a presentation speech.
FOLLOW-UP • If the award is for someone in your class or family, present it in person. If it is for a person who cannot be reached, ask one of your classmates to accept the award on her or his behalf.
© Houghton Mifflin Company. All rights reserved.

Language Workshops
Parts of Speech
Irregular Verbs
Subject-Verb Agreement
Using Colorful Adjectives
Using Conjunctions

Reading and Learning Strategies
SQ3R
Summarizing
KWL
Reading Maps
Using Charts

Talking and Listening Activities
Group Discussions
Presenting an Award
Interviewing a Classmate
Listening for Details

214 *Thinking Workshops*

PARAPHRASING AND INVENTING

FORE • THOUGHT By 1791, two years after the United States Constitution went into effect, the first U.S. Congress had passed 10 amendments (formal additions) to the Constitution. These 10, taken together, are known as the Bill of Rights and guarantee that every citizen of the United States has certain basic liberties: the right to practice one's own religion, the right to speak freely, the right to gather in peaceful groups, and so on.

We the People

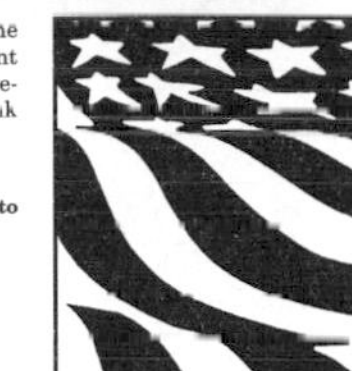

You will find the "Bill of Rights" listed in the index of *Write Source 2000.* Choose the amendment that interests you the most. Read the amendment carefully and discuss with another person what you think it means.

After you thoroughly understand it, "translate" the amendment into modern language that speaks clearly to you.

Translation:

AFTER • THOUGHT What if Congress an… Rights from the Constitution? Imagine what … no freedom of the press, no freedom to assem… imagination. From a student's point of view, … world might be like five years after all the… removed.

Thinking Workshops

Solving Problems
Forming Understanding
Making Decisions
Evaluating
Building Arguments

VOCABULARY AND WORD PLAY ACTIVITIES • 229

WRITING POETRY

A Vision of Poetry

The writers of your handbook talk a lot about using vivid language, "showing" language. They say that your writing should show rather than tell. It should paint a picture in the minds of your readers. Well, there is a kind of poetry that does just that. It's called typographical or concrete poetry. It actually shows and tells at the same time. (Look at the example below.)

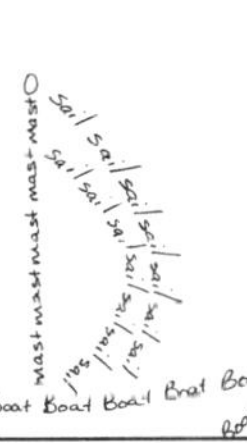

On your own paper, write a typographical poem … face (a self-portrait), it can show you doing somet… favorite sport, or . . . surprise us.

AFTER • WORDS Share your poem with your classmates… larger version of it using colored paper, …

Vocabulary and Word Play Activities

Writing Poetry
Writing Riddles
Using Word Parts

240 MINILESSONS

Less is more. .... *Improving Your Writing* A

■ Don't miss the good advice in section **121**: "Don't use two words—a verb and an adverb—when a single, vivid verb would be better." Read sections **119-121** to understand how to write more vividly and economically. Then study these samples:

The architect *carefully looked over* the blueprints.
The architect **scanned** the blueprints.
The architect **poured over** the blueprints.
That mutt *ran away with* my burrito.
That mutt **filched** my burrito.

Now you TRY IT:

The loaded bleachers *gave out a high-pitched creaking sound.*
The neighborhood mail carrier always *said things under his breath* to passersby.

Diet Plan .... *Improving Your Writing* B

■ Section **123** helps you spot any major weaknesses in your writing. Browse through the five points, but settle on #5.

PRACTICE fixing sentences that start with the empty words "There" or "It." For example, this sentence needs some "fat reduction":

There was a bloodthirsty mosquito that got into my bedroom last night.

To fix it, (1) take out "There," (2) take out the empty verb "was," (3) take out the word "that," (4) use "mosquito" as your new subject, (5) choose a new verb (or use "got") and rebuild the sentence around it.

A bloodthirsty mosquito sneaked into my bedroom last night.

Now USE this same approach to reduce the fat in the following sentences:

It was a passing fire engine that made me swallow my friendship ring.
At last there were some decent cereals that showed up in our cupboard.
There was this bigger kid who stole Trevor's hightops.

Journey to the Center of the Problem .... *Personal Research* C

■ Read and enjoy the *Write Source 2000* tips on doing "Personal Research" (**265-270**). Pay special attention to the four points under "Connecting: Telling Your Research Story" (**270**).

REMEMBER a time in your life when you discovered something for yourself by tracking down the answer, maybe by talking to other people or by reading a book or magazine.

JOT DOWN whatever you remember that fits under the four headings: (1) What I Knew, (2) What I Wanted to Know, (3) What I Found Out, and (4) What I Learned.

Writing and Learning Minilessons

The Process of Writing
The Forms of Writing
The Tools of Learning
The Proofreader's Guide

What is included in each SourceBook Teacher's Edition?

The SourceBook Teacher's Edition for each grade level provides everything teachers need to implement the SourceBook activities. Each edition includes unit teacher's notes, writing frameworks for curriculum planning, a suggested yearlong timetable of lessons, assessment activities, and the appropriate SourceBook answer key.

- Unit Teacher's Notes
- Writing Frameworks
- Yearlong Timetable of Lessons
- Assessment Activities

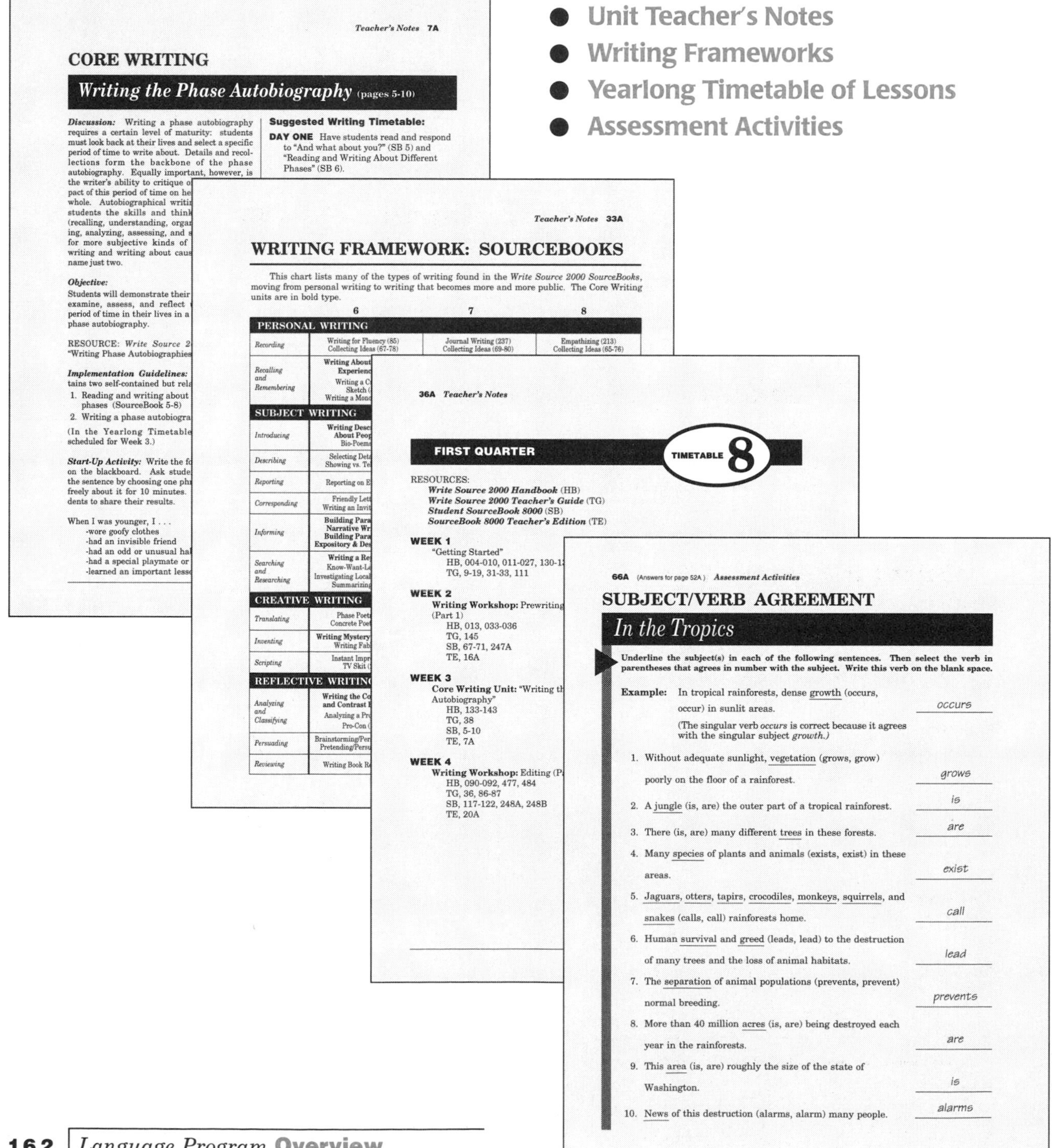

Teacher's Notes **7A**

CORE WRITING

Writing the Phase Autobiography (pages 5-10)

Discussion: Writing a phase autobiography requires a certain level of maturity: students must look back at their lives and select a specific period of time to write about. Details and recollections form the backbone of the phase autobiography. Equally important, however, is the writer's ability to critique o pact of this period of time on he whole. Autobiographical writi students the skills and think (recalling, understanding, orga ing, analyzing, assessing, and s for more subjective kinds of writing and writing about caus name just two.

Objective:
Students will demonstrate their examine, assess, and reflect period of time in their lives in a phase autobiography.

RESOURCE: *Write Source 2* "Writing Phase Autobiographie

Implementation Guidelines: tains two self-contained but rel
1. Reading and writing about phases (SourceBook 5-8)
2. Writing a phase autobiogra

(In the Yearlong Timetable scheduled for Week 3.)

Start-Up Activity: Write the f on the blackboard. Ask stude the sentence by choosing one ph freely about it for 10 minutes. dents to share their results.

When I was younger, I . . .
- -wore goofy clothes
- -had an invisible friend
- -had an odd or unusual ha
- -had a special playmate or
- -learned an important less

Suggested Writing Timetable:

DAY ONE Have students read and respond to "And what about you?" (SB 5) and "Reading and Writing About Different Phases" (SB 6).

Teacher's Notes **33A**

WRITING FRAMEWORK: SOURCEBOOKS

This chart lists many of the types of writing found in the *Write Source 2000 SourceBooks*, moving from personal writing to writing that becomes more and more public. The Core Writing units are in bold type.

	6	7	8
PERSONAL WRITING			
Recording	Writing for Fluency (85) Collecting Ideas (67-78)	Journal Writing (237) Collecting Ideas (69-80)	Empathizing (213) Collecting Ideas (65-76)
Recalling and Remembering	**Writing About ... Experienc...** Writing a C... Sketch ... Writing a Mon...		
SUBJECT WRITING			
Introducing	**Writing Desc... About Peop...** Bio-Poem...		
Describing	Selecting Det... Showing vs. Te...		
Reporting	Reporting on E...		
Corresponding	Friendly Lett... Writing an Invi...		
Informing	**Building Para... Narrative Wr... Building Para... Expository & Des...**		
Searching and Researching	**Writing a Re...** Know-Want-L... Investigating Local... Summarizin...		
CREATIVE WRITING			
Translating	Phase Poet... Concrete Poe...		
Inventing	**Writing Mystery...** Writing Fab...		
Scripting	Instant Impr... TV Skit ...		
REFLECTIVE WRITING			
Analyzing and Classifying	**Writing the Co... and Contrast ...** Analyzing a Pr... Pro-Con ...		
Persuading	Brainstorming/Per... Pretending/Persu...		
Reviewing	Writing Book R...		

36A *Teacher's Notes*

FIRST QUARTER — **TIMETABLE 8**

RESOURCES:
Write Source 2000 Handbook (HB)
Write Source 2000 Teacher's Guide (TG)
Student SourceBook 8000 (SB)
SourceBook 8000 Teacher's Edition (TE)

WEEK 1
"Getting Started"
HB, 004-010, 011-027, 130-1...
TG, 9-19, 31-33, 111

WEEK 2
Writing Workshop: Prewriting (Part 1)
HB, 013, 033-036
TG, 145
SB, 67-71, 247A
TE, 16A

WEEK 3
Core Writing Unit: "Writing th... Autobiography"
HB, 133-143
TG, 38
SB, 5-10
TE, 7A

WEEK 4
Writing Workshop: Editing (P...
HB, 090-092, 477, 484
TG, 36, 86-87
SB, 117-122, 248A, 248B
TE, 20A

66A (Answers for page 52A) *Assessment Activities*

SUBJECT/VERB AGREEMENT

In the Tropics

Underline the subject(s) in each of the following sentences. Then select the verb in parentheses that agrees in number with the subject. Write this verb on the blank space.

Example: In tropical rainforests, dense growth (occurs, occur) in sunlit areas. *occurs*
(The singular verb *occurs* is correct because it agrees with the singular subject *growth.*)

1. Without adequate sunlight, vegetation (grows, grow) poorly on the floor of a rainforest. *grows*
2. A jungle (is, are) the outer part of a tropical rainforest. *is*
3. There (is, are) many different trees in these forests. *are*
4. Many species of plants and animals (exists, exist) in these areas. *exist*
5. Jaguars, otters, tapirs, crocodiles, monkeys, squirrels, and snakes (calls, call) rainforests home. *call*
6. Human survival and greed (leads, lead) to the destruction of many trees and the loss of animal habitats. *lead*
7. The separation of animal populations (prevents, prevent) normal breeding. *prevents*
8. More than 40 million acres (is, are) being destroyed each year in the rainforests. *are*
9. This area (is, are) roughly the size of the state of Washington. *is*
10. News of this destruction (alarms, alarm) many people. *alarms*

What is included in the

Daily Language Workouts?

The Daily Language Workouts for grades 6–8 help students develop their editing and proofreading skills. This flexible teacher's resource includes high-interest language activities that take only a few minutes of class time each day.

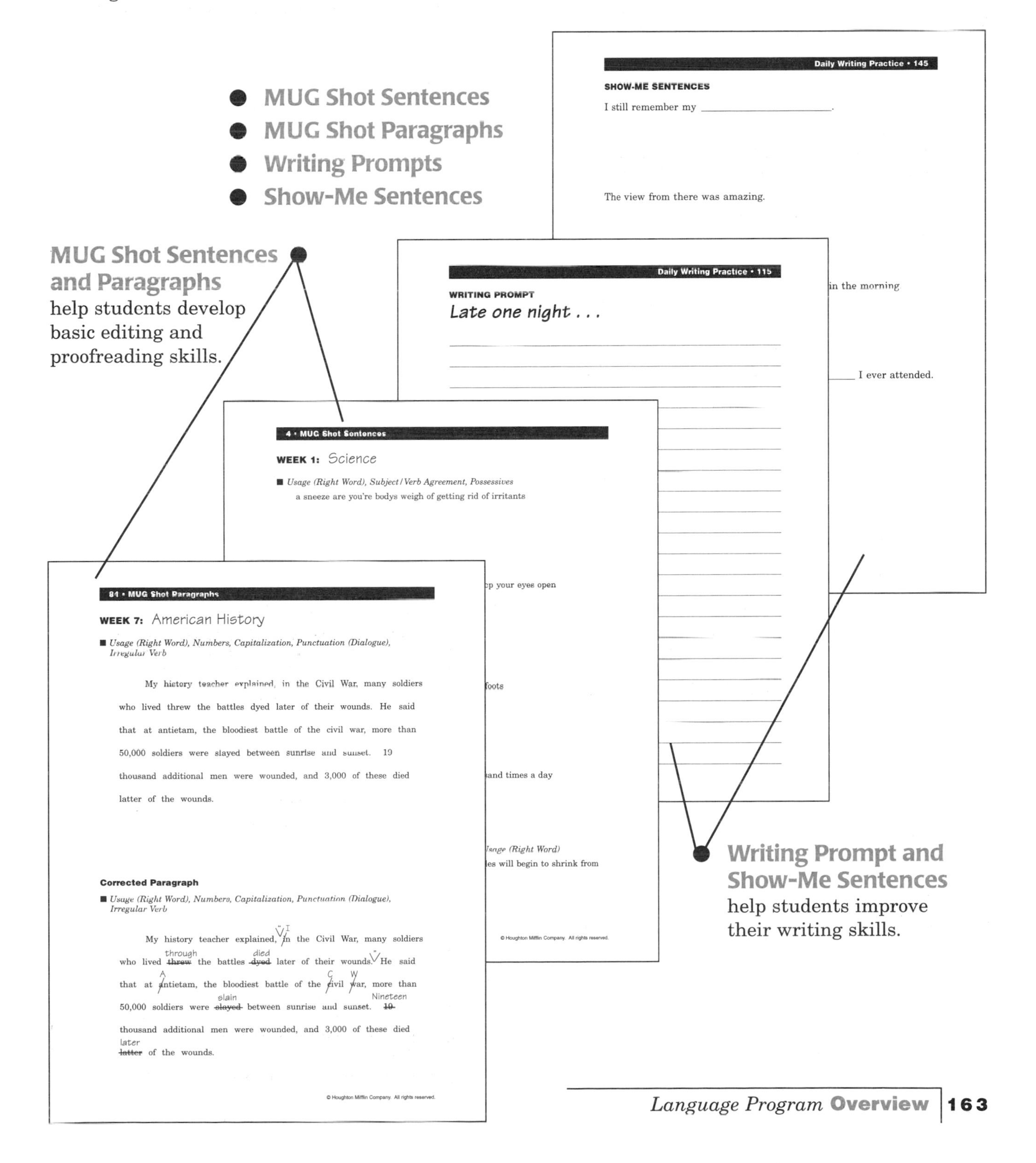

MUG Shot Sentences
MUG Shot Paragraphs
Writing Prompts
Show-Me Sentences
MUG Shot Sentences and Paragraphs help students develop basic editing and proofreading skills.
Writing Prompt and Show-Me Sentences help students improve their writing skills.
Daily Writing Practice • 145
SHOW-ME SENTENCES
I still remember my ________.
The view from there was amazing.
in the morning
____ I ever attended.
Daily Writing Practice • 115
WRITING PROMPT
Late one night . . .
4 • MUG Shot Sentences
WEEK 1: Science
Usage (Right Word), Subject/Verb Agreement, Possessives
a sneeze are you're bodys weigh of getting rid of irritants
p your eyes open
foots
and times a day
Usage (Right Word)
es will begin to shrink from
© Houghton Mifflin Company. All rights reserved.
81 • MUG Shot Paragraphs
WEEK 7: American History
Usage (Right Word), Numbers, Capitalization, Punctuation (Dialogue), Irregular Verb
My history teacher explained, in the Civil War, many soldiers who lived threw the battles dyed later of their wounds. He said that at antietam, the bloodiest battle of the civil war, more than 50,000 soldiers were slayed between sunrise and sunset. 19 thousand additional men were wounded, and 3,000 of these died latter of the wounds.
Corrected Paragraph
Usage (Right Word), Numbers, Capitalization, Punctuation (Dialogue), Irregular Verb
My history teacher explained, "In the Civil War, many soldiers who lived through the battles died later of their wounds." He said that at Antietam, the bloodiest battle of the Civil War, more than 50,000 soldiers were slain between sunrise and sunset. Nineteen thousand additional men were wounded, and 3,000 of these died later of the wounds.
© Houghton Mifflin Company. All rights reserved.

Additional Write Source Products

The following writing resources are all designed to work with *Writers INC*. The series of folders will help students manage all of their writing. The "Personal Writing Books" promote different types of exploratory thinking and writing.

Writing Folders

Laminated, heavy-duty pocket folders are punched for use in three-ring binders.

- **Writing Folders** provide guidelines and advice before, during, and after the writing process. Each folder can also serve as a repository, a portfolio, for work-in-progress as well as completed writing.
- **Punctuation Pockets** will answer anyone's punctuation and capitalization questions. A complete list of rules is printed on the inside and outside of this folder.
- **Topic Folders** offer more than 150 topics for free writing. They also contain an easy-to-use chart that allows students to keep track of their writing progress.

Personal Writing Books

Reflections stimulates and challenges students with thought-provoking ideas, quotations, and photos.

A Daily Journal offers suggestions for starting and maintaining a journal, plus plenty of inviting writing space.

The **Response Journal** provides a place for students to explore their thoughts and feelings about the books they read.

Write in here is a blank personal writing book just waiting to be filled with thoughts and feelings. Use for free writing and journals, early efforts, final drafts, and personal anthologies. *Write in here* also contains a list of free-writing topics and a writing-progress chart.

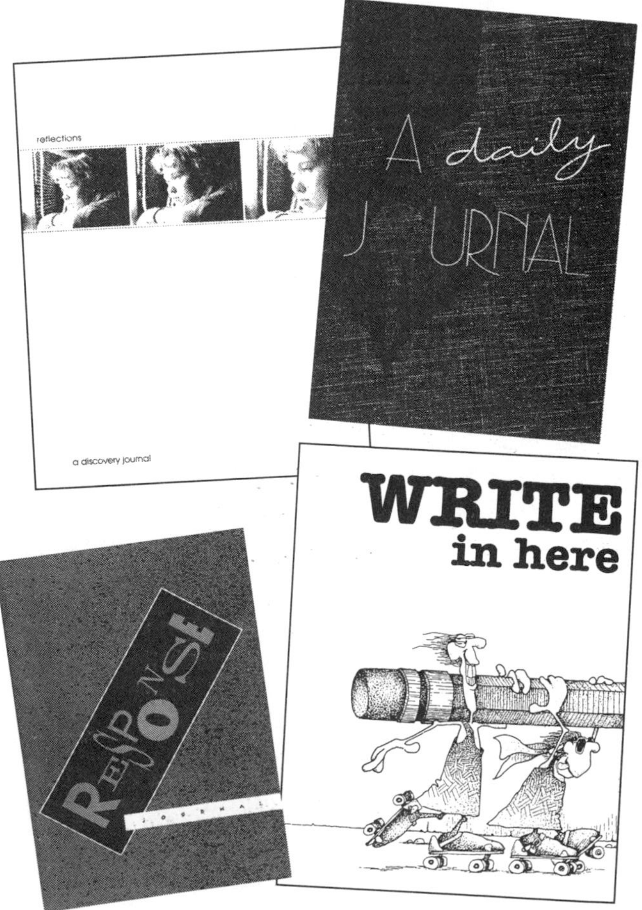

Write Source
Great Source Education Group
Phone 1-800-289-4490

Index

G

H

I

J

K

L

M

N

O

P

Q

R

S